# HOW TO WRITE BETTER SONGS

## SONGWRITING SECRETS FROM AWARD-WINNING SONGWRITERS

---

by **SCOTT ASHLEY**

*Scott Ashley*

Copyright © 2022 Lionheart Productions, Inc. All rights reserved. No part of this book shall be reproduced, stored in a retrieval system, or transmitted by any means without written permission from the author, except for brief quotations in a book review.

How to Write Better Songs: Songwriting Secrets from Award-Winning Songwriters

1st Edition

ISBN: 9798840142196

Lionheart Productions

*How To Write Better Songs*

# CONTENTS

Author's Note ............................................................................. 7
Introduction: Quick Start to Writing a Song ............................ 9
Chapter 1: How to Write a Killer Hook ................................. 13
Chapter 2: How to Write Better Verses ................................. 19
Chapter 3: Tips for Writing a Pre-Chorus .............................. 23
Chapter 4: Tips for Writing a Song Bridge ............................. 25
Chapter 5: Secrets to Writing a Great Chorus ........................ 29
Chapter 6: Ideas for Creating Chord Progressions ................. 33
Chapter 7: Ideas for Writing Great Melodies ......................... 41
Chapter 8: Tips to Use Rhyme to Enhance Your Lyrics ......... 49
Chapter 9: Secrets to Better Storytelling ................................ 59
Chapter 10: How to Write a Melody for Any Lyric ............... 65
Chapter 11: Toplining ............................................................ 71
Chapter 12: Tips to Help You Complete a Song .................... 77
Chapter 13: Beatles Songwriting Secrets I Wish I Knew Earlier ........... 83
Chapter 14: Tips for Entering Songwriting Competitions ...... 93
Chapter 15: Collaborations & Focusing On Your Strengths ... 99
Chapter 16: Sad Truths Why Some Songwriters Never Succeed ........... 105
Chapter 17: Four Types of Music Publishing Royalties ......... 111
Chapter 18: Copyright Your Songs ...................................... 119
Chapter 19: How to Record or Demo Your Songs ............... 125
Conclusion ........................................................................... 129
About the Author ................................................................ 135
Works Cited ......................................................................... 137

*Scott Ashley*

*How To Write Better Songs*

# DEDICATION

This book is dedicated to Jon Aldrich, songwriting professor at the Berklee College of Music in Boston, MA. You are the best!

To songwriters and music makers everywhere, this book is for you.

---

*"It doesn't matter what you do, just go where the music takes you" ~ Ari Gold, the late singer-songwriter*

---

Ari Gold was the Overall Grand Prize winner of the 2007 USA Songwriting Competition for "Where The Music Takes You."

The song debuted at #10 on the Billboard Charts 6 months after winning the USA Songwriting Competition. Ari died of leukemia on February 14, 2021, just three days after his 47th birthday.

*Scott Ashley*

*How To Write Better Songs*

# Author's Note

Songwriting can be very complex and sometimes very challenging. This book helps to you write better songs with advice from award-winning songwriters.

— Scott Ashley

Lionheart Productions

*Scott Ashley*

# Introduction:

# Quick Start to Writing a Song

Are you interested in writing a song? But you don't know where to start? Here are ten simple steps to get you going.

**1. Choose and Compose a Title of your Song**

What sums up the heart of your song's message? You need to come up with a theme for your song to start writing. A good tool is brainstorming song titles.

**2. Write from Experience or Fantasy**

You may wish to brainstorm possible lyrics. It doesn't matter if they don't all fit. What do you want to say through your title? What do you think your listeners might want to know? These are the questions you need to ask yourself. Writing about an experience or feelings is a common way to get started.

**3. Choose a Song Structure**

Currently, the most popular song structure is as follows:

- Verse
- Chorus
- Verse
- Chorus

- Bridge
- Chorus

This songwriting structure formula is ABABCB.

Analyze the structures of your favorite songs. Do they follow the pattern of verse, verse, chorus, and then bridge, or do they just repeat verses and choruses? If your favorite song is "Someone Like You" by Adele, what is the song structure?

**4. Construct a Temporary Chorus and Verse**

What do you want to say in your chorus and hook? Look for imagery and action words that bring your answers to life. What emotions are you describing? What do you wish to say in your verse?

**5. Find the Melody in your Lyric**

Choose the lines you like best for your chorus and hook. Recite them out loud with emotion.

**6. Chord Progression**

Add chords to the melody of your Verses and Chorus. Try a simple, repeated chord pattern. Play around with the melody and chords until you find something you like. I suggest experimenting by singing or humming over the chord progression. You can also use a background music track. Remember, one of the world's biggest hits in recent years was written with a background track — "Old Town Road" by 'Lil Nas X.

## 7. Rhyming

Find pairs of phrases for your Chorus and Hook. Remember to connect the words that rhyme. You can use an internet search to find websites that help find rhymes for words. One is https://www.rhymezone.com. Another free online rhyming dictionary is at https://www.rhymer.com.

## 8. Connect Your Verses and Chorus and Bridge

Connect the melody with your lyrics. Do you want to add a bridge before adding the final chorus? Explore your song's ideas, concepts, and messages, then add new connections through the bridge.

## 9. Intro

Do you need an intro at all, or should the song begin with singing? Keep it short and simple if you need an opening for a mood setter. Many songs on the radio have short intros, and many start with none. Led Zeppelin's long intro on "Stairway to Heaven" was unique. Not many songs can get away with such a long introduction.

## 10. Putting it all together: Record a Demo

A simple guitar and voice recording can be an excellent first step for your song. Or do vocals over an existing music background track. It doesn't need to be perfect at first; you just need to start assembling your song. It is a process, not perfection! [1]

---

[1] (Randle, 10 Simple Steps to Write a Song, 2020)

## Chapter 1:

## How to Write a Killer Hook

There is an art to writing a great chorus with great hooks. The hook and chorus are the most memorable parts of any song, especially since they are repeated several times, sometimes many times. In fact, writing a great hook makes your song stand out from the crowd, magnetically attracting favorable attention and stoking the songwriter or producer's confidence and creativity.

This energy from the hook emanates outward from its center and, in a closed-loop or "boomerang effect," _hooks_ the listener in. This is why composing a great hook is so vital. A good hook will make or break a song.

So, what is a hook? It's a musical idea, often a short riff, passage, or phrase used in Pop, Rock, R&B, or Country music to make a song appealing. It does this by "catching the listener's ear." It's like hooking a fish. Once you set the hook, they're on the line.

Often, people confuse the hook with the chorus, but the hook is not always in the chorus. Sometimes the hook is in the verse, sometimes in the chorus. No rule says where it has to go.

## 1. Rhythm hook

The rhythm hook establishes the beat and rhythm combination (such as a Chord Progression) on which the song is built. Think of "Billie Jean," "Ice, Ice, Baby," "Superstition," "Another One Bites The Dust," "Summer of '69," etc.

In the example of "Billie Jean," one of the most iconic pop songs of all time, the accompaniment is followed by a repetitive three-note synth, played staccato with a deep reverb, establishing the defining rhythmic chord progression. The rest is pop music history. "Billie Jean" became the most definitive song of Michael Jackson's career and established him as the "King of Pop."

How to compose (or write) a Rhythm hook:

   i. Tap your foot
   ii. Compose a short beat rhythm on your guitar or piano that grabs your attention
   iii. Create a chord progression that accompanies the hook (Example: C, F, G)
   iv. Write a bass line that complements the rhythm and chord pattern

## 2. Intro hook

An intro hook is usually a melodic idea established in the introduction. The intro hook makes the song instantly recognizable. Think about "Eye of the Tiger," "Smoke on the Water," "Seven Nation Army," "Layla," and Eric Clapton's "Wonderful Tonight."

"Wonderful Tonight" is a great example. The song opens with its hook, eight measures of Clapton's string-bending soulful guitar, making it one of Pop/Rock's most recognizable iconic Classics. Eric Clapton wrote the ballad for his wife, Pattie Boyd.

How to compose an Intro hook:

i. Compose a short melodic idea on your guitar or piano.
ii. Carefully choose or pick a few music notes
iii. Add a chord progression that follows the notes
iv. Experiment and edit, make changes, repeat.

## 3. Background Instrumental Hook

I believe instrumental hooks are one of the most under-utilized devices in a songwriter's toolbox. They are also one of the most important. Like Ariana Grande's "7 Rings," Ah-Ha's "Take On Me," and Bob Dylan's "Like a Rolling Stone."

With Ariana Grande's "7 Rings," you're likely to think of that catchy single's reverbed synth sound playing half notes, with occasional eighth-note passing notes. Ariana's debut on the Billboard Hot 100 Charts was a massive success, starting in the top spot at #1. It didn't hurt that she repurposed melodic portions of "My Favorite Things" from the classic Julie Andrews movie, *The Sound of Music.*

How to compose a Background Instrumental Hook:

i. Compose chord progression, music notes, etc., on your guitar or piano.
ii. Compose it with the chorus or refrain
iii. Try it with lyrics
iv. Experiment

Here's what award-winning songwriters say about writing a hook:

"The most challenging aspect of writing a great song hook is finding a unique song title and delivering a strong enough melody to guarantee that people will remember it," said Joe Hogue and Sean Petersen, Overall Grand Prize winners of the 2007 USA Songwriting Competition. Their winning song, "Where the Music Takes You," hit #10 on the Billboard Charts, 6 months after winning the Top award.

"Don't just settle for your first hook. Always try to beat it with the next idea. I wrote a song recently where my original chorus hook became the verse hook, and that totally works. Hopefully, that means my verse is now much more catchy and that my chorus is even stronger," said Scott Oatley, Overall Grand Prize winner of the 2021 USA Songwriting Competition.

So, write, rewrite and experiment. Writing a great hook is not easy, but it's worth the time and energy if you are looking to write a great song. [2]

---

[2] (Randle, How to Write a Killer Hook, 2020)

*Scott Ashley*

# Chapter 2:

# How to Write Better Verses

Your goal is to write a song that grabs the listener, making them feel compelled to keep listening.

**1. How to write your first verse**

Create a melody and then write lyrics to match that. Start with solid imagery or imagery that moves in steps, from simple to complicated, from basic to more complex. Example: listen to the first verse of "Someone Like You" by Adele.

*I heard that you're settled down*

*That you found a girl and you're married now*

**2. How to write your second verse**

Remember that songs are short stories. Ask yourself what your song is about and summarize its message. Breaking it into bite-size pieces can often help you move forward into the second verse, a continuation of your story. Remind yourself of the song's message, and you should find a way to continue the story and stay true to the theme.

Take the melody from the first verse and write lyrics that utilize the rhythm pattern and tune you already established but without making it a carbon copy of the first verse. Example: listen to Adele's second verse of "Someone Like You" and notice how she continues her story.

*You know how the time flies*

*Only yesterday was the time of our lives*

**Here's advice from some award-winning songwriters**

"If the first verse is super-busy, a lot of words, maybe the next part should be the complete opposite, with long notes. It's a good resource when you're stuck. But the thing that happens within the method has to be free-flowing and creative in order to be great. That's the magic part," said Max Martin in a Variety magazine interview in 2019.

Max Martin is one of the most successful songwriters today, with 70 US Top 10 hits and 22 No. 1s —including "Baby One More Time" by Britney Spears, Katy Perry's "I Kissed a Girl," Taylor Swift's "Shake It Off," and the Weeknd's "Can't Feel My Face."

"I'd say the easiest way to develop your verses is to simply make sure you know what you're writing about," said Scott Oatley, Overall Grand Prize winner of the 2021 USA Songwriting Competition. "Too often I see other writers start rolling with a vague feeling or thought that just isn't fully developed or realized. You can't write the details of a story if you haven't decided who, what, when, where, why this is all taking place. Decide on your character, point of view, what you want to say (most likely what you end up singing in the chorus!) and fill in the gaps," he said.

Les Sampou, a singer-songwriter as well as a winner of the Lyrics category of the 2021 USA Songwriting Competition, said, "The best verses tell the details of the song, like the facts of a story. The melody and chord progress must support the emotion of the details. The chord progression for the Pre-chorus sets up the chorus to typically there is a build," he said.

"I believe that keeping it simple while writing a song is essential, but it is always a huge challenge for every songwriter," said Meg Pfeiffer, honorable mention winner of the 2021 USA Songwriting Competition. "Sometimes we think too complicated and it is an art to unfold the entire piece first, just to put it back together with a more clear and transparent vision."

"One tip that I have found helpful in writing verses and a pre-chorus is to get visual." Justin Ezzi was the First Prize winner of the Novelty/Comedy category of the 2021 USA Songwriting Competition. He continued, saying, "I often draw a picture of the title. Then in the margins of my drawing, I'll answer who, what, when, how, and why. It's kind of a mind map of what the song is trying to say. It's an interesting exploration because, basically (as a songwriter), I'm trying to paint a picture with words and music. Try it. You'll be amazed at what comes up," he said.

Sonny King, first prize winner of the R&B category in the 2021 USA Songwriting Competition, said, "The verses, in my opinion, are the details of the story. Depending on how the chorus comes together, I want to expand on that concept more in the verses. If the chorus is about how much I'm in love, then the verses will explain why I feel that way. The challenge is to keep the listener engaged in the verse just as much as the chorus, so the song constantly builds with ups and downs. The goal is to take them on an emotional roller coaster with dips and turns and a surprise ending!"

# Chapter 3:

# Tips for Writing a Pre-Chorus

A pre-chorus is an optional song section that joins the verse with the chorus. Not every song needs one, but you'll want to consider a pre-chorus if:

1. the verse and chorus melodies are very similar-sounding;
2. the verse is short;
3. the chord progression of the verse is short, perhaps only one or two chords;
4. the chorus melody sits a lot higher in pitch than the verse melody;
5. the energy of the chorus is dramatically higher than that of the verse.

Create a melody and write lyrics to it. For example, listen to the pre-chorus of "Someone Like You" by Adele:

*I hate to turn up out of the blue, uninvited*

*But I couldn't stay away, I couldn't fight it*

Here is some advice from award-winning songwriter Scott Oatley, Overall Grand Prize winner of the 2021 USA Songwriting Competition, about writing verses and pre-chorus:

"As far as a pre-chorus goes, I just try to change it up with something interesting (chord-wise, melody-wise, rhythm-wise) that gets us from point A (the verse) to point B (the chorus). Don't overcomplicate it," he said.

"You don't always need a pre-chorus; it depends on the song," said Jeff Roe, honorable mention winner of the 2021 USA Songwriting Competition. "I've also used a pre-chorus for the first verse only and not for each verse. One thing I try to do melodically is to not end on too high of a note. This gives you room to let your chorus soar! I like to think of the pre-chorus like a golfer teeing up his shot and swinging for that big chorus moment … bam!"

"Melodically, my verses tend to have faster rhythms than the chorus. The verse, from a lyrical perspective, is where your story is established and moves," said Jamie Alimorad, Overall Grand Prize winner of the 2019 USA Songwriting Competition with co-writer Gino Vannelli.

Alimorad continued, "That first line is very important to me. I want to hook you right away with something compelling, something that instantly lets you know you're in for a ride. The pre-chorus is where I like to provide a lift. It's that subliminal notice that we're moving somewhere else, and then when you get to the chorus, it lands that much harder," he said.

# Chapter 4:

# Tips for Writing a Song Bridge

A bridge's primary purpose is to create contrast from the rest of the song. But not every song needs a bridge; it all depends on how the song feels.

For review: contemporary songs usually have at least three sections – the verse, the chorus, and the bridge – but it's not a hard and fast rule. Ideally, for each section, the melody line, chords, rhythm, and words are different from each other. Whatever you've done in the verse, don't do it in the chorus or the bridge, and whatever you do in the chorus, don't do it in the verse or the bridge. If you find you overlap or borrow from earlier parts of your song, revise the bridge, so you don't.[3]

Create a melody and new chord progression for your bridge that explores an "opposite mode" from the chorus. Now write lyrics to it. Example: listen to the bridge of "Someone Like You" by Adele:

*Nothing compares, no worries or cares*

*Regrets and mistakes, they're memories made*

---

[3] (Leikin, 2013)

Here's what award-winning songwriters are saying about writing bridges:

"We always like to think of the bridge as being something unexpected. It could be the lyrics, it could be the chord changes, it could be the sounds, or it could be the melody, but usually, we are trying to surprise the listener in this section, hopefully making them think. The Bridge is the section of the song that should include the exclamation point! We want the *listener* to *want* to repeat the song after hearing the bridge," said Joe Hogue and Sean Petersen, Overall Grand Prize co-winners of the 2007 USA Songwriting Competition. Their winning song with co-writer and late music artist Ari Gold, "Where the Music Takes You," debuted at #10 on the Billboard Charts, 6 months after winning the Top award.

Scott Oatley, Overall Grand Prize winner of the 2021 USA Songwriting Competition, said, "I'd say the first question to ask, especially with today's music, is "Does this song even need a bridge?" Traditionally, the bridge gives us a fresh break from the chorus and introduces some new idea or further clarity that ties the whole song together.' Oakley continued, "But if you've already said everything there is to say, just sing that chorus one more time and get out of there! Then make your listeners stream the song again."

"The bridge is my favorite part of a song," said Jamie Alimorad, Overall Grand Prize winner of the 2019 USA Songwriting Competition with co-writer Gino Vannelli. "A good bridge will surprise you, and take you somewhere unexpected. Maybe you go to the relative or hit a secondary dominant. If you think of it from a literary point of view, the verses and the early choruses are the conflict in the story. The bridge is the solution and changes the meaning of the chorus for the outro. From all areas, a great bridge will excite you and build that energy before landing in the final chorus."

"More and more bridges are disappearing from pop songs. I find that to be a shame," added Alimorad. "The challenge of the bridge is to write something surprising without straying too far from the core of the song, or just being contrived. This is the moment in the song where the storyteller, both in the musical and lyrical sense, really comes out," he said.

"I don't use bridges unless there's something else I haven't already said in the verses and chorus that will add to the song," according to Jeff Roe, honorable mention winner of the 2021 USA Songwriting Competition. "If you do have a bridge, make sure every line points to the hook, and the last line sets up the chorus again and shines a light on the hook in a new and interesting way you haven't already used in the verses."

"A bridge should change the feel of the song. I often use the bridge to slow or speed up the feel depending on where the tempo has been up to this point. Lyrically, a new message, a counter-message, appears in the bridge. Something perhaps a bit more revealing, or a question," said Les Sampou, a singer-songwriter as well as a winner of the Lyrics category of the 2021 USA Songwriting Competition.

"Writing the bridge can be challenging, but it's always fun for me because it's a chance to really drive home the message of the entire song and leave that final impression on the listener that makes them say, "I have to listen to this again," said Sonny King, first prize winner of the R&B category in the 2021 USA Songwriting Competition. "I also use the bridge as a way to increase excitement in the song. I like to create a different chord progression, in the same song key, of course, that brings us towards that climatic close. It's like a surprise right before the ending for the listener."

King continued, "Lyrically, I want to expand on the story with something that reiterates the message or adds a new perspective to the conversation. This is my last chance to leave a lasting impression on them before the final chorus. I think another way to look at it is to ask yourself was there anything left unsaid. Did I answer all the questions?"

# Chapter 5:

# Secrets to Writing a Great Chorus

The chorus is the "heart" of the song. It is the part of the song when your audience can't wait to reach that catchy Chorus with melodic and lyric hooks.

A song's chorus will be more memorable if it's also emotionally moving. Choruses can be angry, sad, affectionate, or playful—any state of mind can inspire a song.

**1. Melody**

This is the most critical part of the song; it is your statement. If the melody isn't strong, your chorus will suffer accordingly. A contrast of melody from the verse can make your song stand out. For example, in Dolly Parton's biggest hit song, "I Will Always Love You," the chorus is a stark contrast to the verse. The melody in the chorus is thinner and makes the chorus stand out more than the verse. In your song, you can use wide intervals, long tones, short rhythms, or different melodic rhythms to make it stand out from the verse.

**2. Lyrics**

What do you want to remain at the forefront for your audience? You always want to remind your listeners what your song's about. Lyrics can be tricky because they should summarize the song's overall theme and mood. A good example is "Since U Been Gone" by Kelly Clarkson, written by Max Martin and Lukasz Gottwald, aka "Dr. Luke." The lyrics include, "Since U Been Gone, I can breathe for the first time, I'm so moving on, yeah yeah." The lyrics make it memorable for the listener, something that resonates with them, and they can identify with it.

## 3. Use Your Hook

The hit song "I Hate Myself for Loving You" by Joan Jett and the Blackhearts, written by Desmond Child and Kenny Laguna, uses the hook intro to incorporate the chorus – a clever choice that brings the listener in. Remember, you can use your hook in your chorus.

## 4. Contrast the Chorus's Melody with a Different Range and Feel

The chorus can be higher in pitch and range, but not always. For example, look at the Nilsson song, "Without You," written by Pete Ham and Tom Evans of the rock band "Badfinger." The chorus provides big sweeping melodies and color, in stark contrast to the verse. Another example is "All By Myself," written and recorded by Eric Carmen. Notice how different the chorus is from the verse in pitch, emotion, and instrumentation. The initial verse is just piano and voice, but the chorus brings in percussion and strings and soars along on the song's hook.

## 5. Know When You Need a Chorus

There are times that you do not need a chorus at all. Then you need is a refrain: a short hook that gets tacked on like "You needed me, you needed me" in Anne Murray's #1 Hit Song, "You Needed Me," written by Randy Goodrum. There's no chorus in that song, just a short refrain, but that's all it needs.

An example of a good chorus is "Best Worst Day Ever" by Justine Dorsey and Kerris Dorsey (Overall Grand prize winner of USA Songwriting Competition in 2014). The song went on to be featured in the movie *Alexander and the Terrible, Horrible, No Good, Very Bad Day,* starring Steve Carell and Jennifer Garner. The chorus is catchy with good play on words.

Another example of a good chorus is "We Make the Way By Walking" by David Wilcox (Overall Grand Prize winner of the USA Songwriting Competition in 2018). The song starts with the chorus – no intro – and grabs the listener's attention from the get-go.

"Now here's the secret about the chorus … it must be "catchy." It must have a good hook simply because most people remember a song by its chorus," according to Wilbur "B52" Levans, First Prize winner in the Hip-Hop category of the 2021 USA Songwriting Competition.

"A chorus is typically where I land my title. A chorus is where the main hook melodically and lyrically lives. It is what you want the listener to remember as well as to be singable and unforgettable," said Les Sampou, a singer-songwriter as well as a winner of the Lyrics category of the 2021 USA Songwriting Competition.

"I always think of an interview with the members of Def Leppard talking about their work with Mutt Lange. They recalled how Lange would say think of the verse as a chorus, think of the pre-chorus as a better chorus, and think of the chorus as the best chorus. That's how you get hits. Every piece of the song is catchy, memorable, and hooky. You want the chorus to be something everyone can sing along with and never forget," said Jamie Alimorad, Overall Grand Prize winner of the 2019 USA Songwriting Competition with co-writer Gino Vannelli.

"If you're aiming for that earworm, less is more. I typically will have more dotted notes, ties, and quarter notes in the chorus compared to the verse. The chorus is your moment. Let it be the thing that no one can get out of their head," added Jamie Alimorad.

So, experiment with your chorus, write and re-write it until you get it the way you want. Remember that it's progress and not perfection! [4]

---

[4] (Randle, 5 Secrets to Writing a Great Chorus, 2020)

# Chapter 6:

# Ideas for Creating Chord Progressions

Songwriting can be a struggle. There's not a set strategy for crafting the next big hit. The chords you use can make all the difference.

Whether a chord progression pro or a songwriting newbie, you can get crafty with chords in many different ways. So here are seven essential tips that'll help you strike the right (pardon me) chord.[5]

*WARNING: Music Theory Ahead.*

**How to Write a Chord Progression**

If finding the best chord progression makes you feel lost, don't beat yourself up! Many songwriters find adding chords to their verses, choruses, and melodies challenging.

I would suggest singing or humming over a potential chord progression to experiment. You could try a simple, repeated chord pattern and then play with the melody and chords until you find something you like. You can also use a backing track.

---

[5] (DittoMusic, 2022)

Once you've got the chord progressions down, find out how to write a song so you can start using them in action!

But for now, check out these seven tips for writing a hit-worthy chord progression.

## 1. Beg, Borrow and Steal

Some song elements are not generally protected under copyright rules, and chord progressions fall into that category. It's OK to take progressions you like in other songs and use them in your own, with certain provisions.

For example, if you like U2's "With or Without You," you can use the same chord progression or play it in a different key to differentiate it from the original song.

This might resemble a change from the original chord progression of D-A-Bm-G to C-G-Am-F.

However, keep in mind that if you feel compelled to borrow more than just the chords—employing the tempos, rhythms, and basic sound of the progression as it exists in someone else's song—you're straying into a dangerous area where you could be guilty of copyright infringement.

We've learned this lesson from the Robin Thicke/Pharrell Williams situation with "Blurred Lines" and from George Harrison's "My Sweet Lord" comparison with the Chiffons' "He's So Fine" before that. Be sure your treatment of the chords you borrow is genuinely yours.

I recommend you change it up a little (or a lot) so your song doesn't sound too similar to the original chord progression. Try altering things like the instrumentation or the primary hook to change it.

**2. Take an Existing Progression and Try it Backward**

Not every progression works when you play it backward, but sometimes enough of it works that it will work as a new starting point.

Played backward, the chords in a progression have a different relationship, and sometimes that works, and sometimes it doesn't. But if your ideas are drying up, it's worth trying!

**3. Create Chord Progression Palindromes**

A palindrome usually refers to a word or a phrase that reads the same in both directions. For example, "Madam, I'm Adam."

Similarly, some chord progressions will work well if you switch direction in the middle and finish it in reverse. Something simple like C-F-G---|G-F-C---|.

The longer the progression, the trickier it can be, so you'll want to experiment to discover for yourself what works. Here's a more complex example of a palindromic progression (try 2 beats per chord): C-Am-Em-F|Bb-F-Em-Am|C...

## 4. Use the Circle of Fifths

The Circle of Fifths (aka the Circle of Fourths) is a central concept in music. It outlines the relationship between each of the 12 notes in the chromatic scale and their related Major and minor keys.

The closer two keys are in the Circle of Fifths, the more related they are (i.e., the more notes they share in common). The song "Heart and Soul" is based on a standard circle of fifths progression: C Am Dm G

To get you started, picture a clock face where the C major chord (or A minor) is at the 12 o'clock position. Each number in the clockwise direction is the chord that's a fifth higher. Going in the opposite direction, each chord is a fifth lower.

Look at most chord progressions, and you'll see that this fifth relationship is very important, strengthening the overall progression.

A great example: C-F-Dm-G-C. Most of the adjacent chords are fifth away from each other: C to F, Dm to G, and G to C.

A quick way to use the circle of fifths is to play a C, then play any other chord that naturally exists in C major. From there, move backward (counterclockwise) through the circle until you reach C again.

Let's say you decide to play Em after C. Using the circle, you'd follow that Em with Am, then Dm, then G, and end on C: C-Em-Am-Dm-G-C

## 5. Use a Bass Pedal Point

A pedal point is the repetition or sustaining of a single note through various harmonic changes.

It can make a standard progression sound more exciting or ground a complex progression in something familiar.

Here's an example of a pedal point chord progression: Dm7/G, A7/G, Fmaj7/G, G. The G is the pedal point, anchoring the entire progression.

This doesn't create a new progression for you, but if you've come up with a passage that sounds disorganized or overly complex, keeping your bass sitting on one note – usually the tonic note – adds a musical glue to the progression, strengthening it.

Here's another example. This progression might sound a bit complex: C-Ab|Db-Eb|F-Bb|D-Db|C

Play the progression again, but keep a steady C in the bass. That bass C anchors everything and keeps the listeners' minds riveted on the key of the progression, C major.

A bass pedal point works for any progression, and some great bands, like Genesis, have used them abundantly.

## 6. Use Non-Diatonic Chords

A non-diatonic chord does not exist naturally in the key you've chosen.

For example, in the progression C-F-Fm-C, the Fm is a non-diatonic chord because Fm doesn't exist naturally in C major.

Another example: In the key of A major, the seven naturally-occurring chords are: A, Bm, C#m, D, E, F#m, and G#dim.

Non-diatonic chords are an excellent way to take a simple progression and add a nice splash of color. It can make an ordinarily mundane progression sound fresher and more innovative.

Some other non-diatonic chords to try (with examples from C major): Flat-III (Eb), Flat-VII (Bb), ii-dim (Ddim).

## 7. Use Modes of Your Progression

A modal progression could best be described this way: a set of chords that points to a note other than the tonic (key) note.

In other words, if you're using chords from the key of A major, but the progression _seems_ to be pointing to a different note as the most significant one, you're probably using modal progressions.

This is D Lydian: D E D E D F#m C#m7 D

This is E Mixolydian: E Bm A Bm7 E

Here's what award-winning songwriters are saying about chord progressions:

"I usually start with the lyric and (some) melody ideas and then find chord progressions to put underneath," said 1998 USA Songwriting Competition Overall Grand Prize winner Steffani Bennett. She added, "This particular song was very personal, so it flowed pretty naturally as I recall."

Sonny King, first prize winner in the R&B category of the 2021 USA Songwriting Competition, went into greater detail talking about chord progressions. "The chord progression usually leads me to a melody," he said. "I like to make short phone recordings humming melodies I hear that give me that certain feeling. I have a habit of hearing the chorus melody first and begin the story from there."

He continued, "I feel the chorus is the summary of the entire story and the part of the song that is usually the first thing a listener remembers. I find the chorus is the easier part of the writing process as long I don't overthink it, which can make the process more challenging. I want to be creative and witty but not so complex that it's not memorable. I think a little bit of simplicity and a great melody that you can easily remember goes a long way in building a great chorus."

Sonny had this advice, "I always tell artists to examine the greats that came before us like Prince. Purple Rain is an all-time classic, and the chorus is simple with a great melody and is extremely memorable! The song obviously has a deeper meaning, but it was explained with simplicity. I love the concept that less is more, and there is an art to using just enough to tell the story accurately (while) still making it catchy and easy to sing along with," he said.

Songs with complex chords sound like they're taking you on a musical journey. But at the same time, it's possible to get too wrapped up trying to create an original progression that no one else has ever attempted. The complexity or simplicity of a sequence does not make or break a song. When songs sound great, it's almost always because of the combined strength of the lyrics and melodies. And, at the production level, the power of the performance.

Thus, it *is* possible to worry too much about chords. Use a simpler progression you know will work rather than trying to create a complex progression that leaves your listeners wondering what's going on.

However, suppose your ideas for chords have truly dried up. In that case, hopefully, one of the seven suggestions in this chapter will benefit you. [6]

---

[6] (Ewer, 2021)

# Chapter 7:

# Ideas for Writing Great Melodies

As a songwriter, finding a great melody is like a miner spotting a flake of gold in the bottom of his pan. It doesn't guarantee a great song or a gold strike, but it increases the chances. In this chapter, we'll show you the best spots to dig on Music Mountain in hopes of finding a great melody!

A melody is how a listener remembers the song, lyrics, and even the artist. We can get away with shared use in our drumming patterns, bass lines, and chord progressions, but melodies must be unique! While a melody is defined as a musically satisfying sequence of single notes of various pitches and lengths, the arrangement—the melody—is much more than just notes and rests.

Here are ten ideas – ten tools, if you will – to help you find and enhance your next great melody.

**1. Scales and Intervals**

A thesaurus of musical scales is your best friend. *(Note: an actual thesaurus of music scales does not exist. I looked.—ed.)* Try playing new scales, boring scales, and exotic scales. Play the notes in ascending and descending order initially to get the feel of the scale, then start experimenting. If you are going to sing, play scales in keys and modes that balance with your voice. Pay attention to the intervals of the notes. There are many great videos of famous songs and the intervals used.

## 2. Chords and Arpeggios

A memorable melody is often the overlying chords of the song arpeggiated—played one note at a time. Like scales and intervals, having a solid idea of how chords are built will help you with melody construction. Knowing which chords in a key are tonic, dominant, and more, you can convey the proper emotion, tension, and resolution in your song. Scales and chords can frequently show the way if you're stuck on which note to use next.

## 3. Chord Progressions

When chords are combined in a particular order or sequence, it is called a chord progression. Every genre of music has its own common progressions. Most songs have been composed from only a handful of common progressions. Becoming familiar with those progressions will help you look for a progression that fits your new song idea.

A great way to start a new song is to simply pick a progression and start playing it. Add chord extensions, substitutions, and key modulations, and you'll create some fresh ideas.

## 4. Rhythms and Meters

Experimenting with different time signatures and rhythms is very easy in our age of apps and handheld devices. It is possible to download to your phone or tablet software with drum machines, backing grooves, and every rhythm you could imagine. Look up different time signatures and genres, then play your scales and chord progressions over the new settings. If you struggle with music theory, this is your best step. Find a backing tempo, rhythm, track, or any music without a melody, and start jamming. For aspiring hip-hop artists, a drum machine or sampler is your sketchpad.

## 5. Change Your Sound

Try different instruments, effects, and new technology. Many famous songs were written when bands found new toys in the studio to play with. Try out a new instrument at a jam, especially one from another instrument family. Synthesizers and computer-driven music are great because they can give you different sound effects and abilities.

These days, synths are associated with EDM (electronic dance music) and home music production, but some of the best songwriters love synthesizers' ability to create new original sounds. A great melody needs creativity; changing your perspective is part of that.

## 6. Steps and Skips

So far, we have mostly gone over melody inspiration methods. However, there are some basic rules when writing a melody.

Moving up or down the scale one note is called a *step*, while moving more than one step is a *skip* or a *leap*. Usually, we move stepwise – like going up or down a staircase – because that is the easiest way for most people to sing. However, our song also needs skips and leaps to make it interesting and exciting. Play your intervals again and check how large a leap you can make vocally; that will help you keep your melodies realistic.

## 7. Song Structure

Along with the note movement, the melody structure of the song is crucial. Sometimes, simple features like shorter notes in the verse or chorus make the song unique. Raising the pitch of the chorus is standard, as is adding a climactic note change as a lead-in to the chorus.

One way to make simple melodies better is with more transitions. Don't just shift from verse to chorus and back to verse; add a bridge or a pre-chorus with a slightly altered melody. Some songs are best known for their bridge or some other small section that sets off the verse or chorus in a new way. A key change can build excitement for a repeated refrain or a final verse, chorus, and ending.

## 8. Repetition

If you are writing your average pop song, you definitely want to repeat the best hook of your melody. Regardless of the genre, the tune is where repetition lives. Even with a good hook, you will find using many of the same notes make it easier to sing. It is common in many great choruses to see repeated notes with a couple short leaps added for interest.

The average pop song may only use a half-dozen notes to build the verse and just a few more for the chorus. Think of running up a staircase partway and coming back down or going up three steps, coming back two, and then going three more before jumping back to the bottom. That's a simple example of a verse. For the chorus, jump up five steps before starting to go up higher by single steps.

We say melodies are more special than other repetitive aspects like the drums, but in reality, a great tune relies on sounds people hear regularly. It also depends on the songwriter keeping it simple enough that the average person can sing along. Ultimately, we all want the world to sing along with our songs.

## 9. Mind the Lyrics

We focus so much on the musical aspect that we forget that many songwriters start with a lyrical approach.

Sometimes the lyrics and music arrive at the same creative moment, while other times, we agonize over the melody or struggle for the right words to fit the melody.

A common mistake is cramming too many words into a line or the wrong number of syllables. Just like some notes sound weird together, so do some consonants and words. If your melody has lyrics, people need to be able to sing the notes and words without getting tongue-tied.

A hard-to-sing tune can make it less accessible to the public, even if they love to hear you sing it. People *like* to sing along with the radio, which helps a song's popularity.

A funny thing that comes out of poor pronunciation or words that don't fit together properly is a mondegreen—aka misheard lyrics. Elton John seems to have a bunch. "Hold me closer, tiny dancer" has been heard countless times as "Hold me closer, Tony Danza." Some others from Elton's songs:

- Had an old dog, Sammy, and a place for my chew
- Goodbye, Aubergine
- Goodbye, normal jeans
- Rocket man burning up his shoes with air
- He's a spitball wizard
- When Suzie watches "Dick Van Dyke"
- She has electric b--bs; her mom has, too

Word choice and *enunciation* are essential.

## 10. Copy and Learn

Listen and replicate what you hear. That's how music works. We hear someone play something, get excited, and want to copy it. Listen to songs you like and figure out the hook or riff. Play as many songs as possible on your instrument of choice and focus on the melody. As you see how successful songwriters do it, eventually, you will figure it out for yourself. Practice different genres; sit down and write a cantastoria murder mystery, a troubadour love song, or a dark funeral dirge. Jump right into music by copying what other musicians have done (but not exact copies!).

This is how great melodies are born. We take what we love and are inspired by and then let our creativity take hold. And if we practice our craft enough, we can find melodies of gold just waiting to be placed in the right song.

"The challenge to writing a great chorus is not getting too busy. Simpler is better in the chorus," said Jamie Alimorad, Overall Grand Prize winner of the 2019 USA Songwriting Competition with co-writer Gino Vannelli.

"Sometimes it can be hard to really know what you want to say, and the chorus becomes a jumbled mess. If you're aiming for that hit, you want to find something unique, but (still) familiar," Alimorad said. "Don't drive yourself crazy to find something memorable. Often that's what will work against you."

*Scott Ashley*

# Chapter 8:

# Tips to Use Rhyme to Enhance Your Lyrics

Rhyme is one of the most effective tools a songwriter can use to make their work stand out. A classic mnemonic device, the rhyme makes your song more memorable while adding structure and uniformity to your work. But figuring out what to rhyme and how can be tricky. Check out these pointers for using rhyme to enhance your lyrics!

**End Rhyme Schemes**

When you think of rhyming, you probably immediately think of end rhymes – where two or more lines of a poem or song have the same end sound. This is the most common form of rhyming in songwriting and, when done effectively, really sets your song apart.

When listening to different songs, you'll notice a few different patterns of end rhymes—rhyming schemes. Here are a few examples of common end rhyme schemes you can use in your lyrics.

Rhyme Scheme: AABB

In this scheme, the first two lines of lyrics share a rhyme, while the following two lines share another. A good example is Coldplay's "Viva La Vida."

*I used to rule the world*
*Seas would rise when I gave the word*
*Now in the morning I sleep alone*
*Sweep the streets I used to own*

This is an easy rhyme scheme to master and is particularly useful for writing choruses and hooks of songs!

Rhyme Scheme: AAAA

This scheme, also called monorhyme, has all four lines sharing the same rhyme. This rhyme scheme can be a little trickier because it requires you to think of more words that sound the same, but it is an excellent tool for building drama in a song. You can see this rhyme scheme in Bruce Springsteen's "Shackled and Drawn."

*Shackled and drawn, shackled and drawn*
*Pick up the rock, son, carry it on*
*We're trudging through the dark in a world gone wrong*
*I woke up this morning shackled and drawn*

## Rhyme Scheme: ABAB

Also known as alternate rhyme, the ABAB pattern is another conventional lyrical rhyme scheme. It rhymes alternating lines with one another – for instance, in Peter Gabriel's song "Solsbury Hill."

*Climbing up on Solsbury Hill*

*I could see the city light*

*Wind was blowing, time stood still*

*Eagle flew out of the night*

## Rhyme Scheme: XAXA

One last common end rhyme scheme involves two lines that don't rhyme, alternating with two that do. You can hear this rhyme scheme in The Beatles' "Let It Be."

*When I find myself in times of trouble*

*Mother Mary comes to me*

*Speaking words of wisdom*

*Let it be*

## Unexpected Rhyme Schemes

Most audiences expect the common end rhyme schemes we listed above, but some rhyme schemes are designed to give listeners something unexpected. For instance, Coldplay uses an AAAB rhyme scheme in their hit song "Fix You." In this pattern, there are three consecutive lines that rhyme, followed by one that doesn't:

*When you try your best but you don't succeed*

*When you get what you want but not what you need*

*When you feel so tired but you can't sleep*

*Stuck in reverse*

Another excellent example of this unexpected rhyme scheme is in Evanescence's "My Immortal."

*When you cried I'd wipe away all of your tears,*

*When you'd scream I'd fight away all of your fears,*

*And I held your hand through all of these years,*

*But you still have all of me*

Notice that the fourth line has a different number of syllables in both of these examples than the previous three lines. This adds another unexpected element to the lyrical (and rhythmic) structure.

**Six Line Schemes**

So far, all of the rhyme schemes we've examined are designed for groups of four lines. But, you can make your lyrics more complex by organizing them into lines of six.

Here are a few rhyme schemes designed for groups of six.

## Rhyme Scheme: AABBAA

In this pattern, the first, second, fifth, and sixth lines rhyme, while the third and fourth lines share a different rhyme. This classic rhyme scheme is often employed in twelve-bar blues and classic rock - as in The Clash's "Should I Stay Or Should I Go?"

*Darling, you've got to let me know*

*Should I stay or should I go?*

*If you say that you are mine*

*I'll be here 'til the end of time*

*So you've got to let me know*

*Should I stay or should I go?*

## Rhyme Scheme: AABCCB

This rhyme scheme breaks the six lines of lyrics into two groups of three rather than into three groups of two. A timeless example of this scheme is in Leonard Cohen's "Hallelujah."

*I heard there was a secret chord*

*That David played, and it pleased the Lord*

*But you don't really care for music, do ya?*

*It goes like this, the fourth, the fifth,*

*The minor fall and the major lift,*

*Scott Ashley*

*The baffled king composing Hallelujah*

**Slant Rhymes**

A common trap songwriters fall into is thinking that all their rhymes must be exact or "true" rhymes - for instance, "might, right, sight, night." Often, however, words that sound similar, but aren't true rhymes, are perfectly acceptable. As long as the words have similar vowels, they can achieve that lyrical smoothness that songwriters strive for. For instance, "sleep" isn't an exact rhyme for "succeed" and "need," but Coldplay rhymes these words with one another in their song "Fix You."

Slant rhymes are necessary because there are a limited number of exact rhymes in the English language. If you only use exact rhymes, your lyrics will all end up very similar and might bore your audience.

**Alliteration**

Although traditional rhymes share sounds at the end of words, you can also use other types of rhymes in your lyrics. One particularly effective type is alliteration or head rhyme. Alliteration involves grouping together multiple words that begin with the same letter or sound.

A great example of alliteration is in the song "Helplessly Hoping" by Crosby, Stills, & Nash.

*How To Write Better Songs*

*Helplessly hoping, her harlequin hovers nearby*

*Awaiting a word*

And later in the song:

*Wordlessly watching, he waits by the window and wonders*

*At the empty place inside*

The repeated beginning letters create a beautiful lyrical flow and make for a truly memorable song.

**Internal Rhyme**

Not all of your rhymes have to be at the ends of phrases. Lots of effective rhyming can be done within individual lyrical lines. This is demonstrated masterfully in Bruce Springsteen's song "Blinded by the Light," which uses a combination of internal rhyme as well as an AABB end rhyme scheme:

*Madman drummers, bummers, and Indians in the summer with a teenage diplomat,*

*In the dumps with the mumps as the adolescent pumps his way into his hat,*

*With a boulder on my shoulder feeling kinda older I tripped the merry-go-round,*

*With this very unpleasing sneezing and wheezing the calliope crashed to the ground.*

Internal rhyme is also very evident in hip-hop music, such as in songs by Eminem and Kendrick Lamar.

**Combine Rhyme Schemes**

Using multiple rhyme schemes in your songwriting will make your songs memorable and fun to listen to. For really compelling lyrics, don't feel limited to one rhyme scheme. Most songs employ at least two schemes, often one for the verses and another for the chorus.

**Know When Not To Rhyme**

Rhyme is a remarkable songwriting tool, but it's not strictly necessary. One mistake songwriters often make is forcing the content of their song to fit into a rhyme scheme rather than the other way around. Your lyrics should convey a story or message with emotion behind them. If the story and emotion are lost by trying to make it rhyme, take the rhyme out. [7]

Here's a tip from award-winning songwriter Mary Beth Stone, honorable mention winner in the 2019 USA Songwriting Competition:

"Make sure always that there's something of yourself in every song you write, even if you're writing about experiences

---

[7] (Randle, Top 8 Tips To Use Rhyme To Enhance Your Lyrics, 2020)

you've never had. If you are connected emotionally to the song, the listener will connect to it also."

*Scott Ashley*

## Chapter 9:

## Secrets to Better Storytelling

Legendary songwriters like Dolly Parton and Bob Dylan know the secret. A killer story is a must to get people to <u>really</u> listen to your song. Of course, for many, songwriting is challenging enough. Now you're expected to write a story, too? Luckily, a few tips can help you craft the perfect story. Here are some songwriting secrets for creating better stories.

**Write Lots of Lists**

New, exciting things happen to you every day. Okay, maybe not everything that happens to you is exciting. Still, it could be enough inspiration to launch your next storytelling song. Keeping lists is the best way to remember all the exciting(ish) events that happen to you.

Before starting your next song, write a list of events that happened to you throughout your life. You don't have to list everything (that would be quite the list). Focus on events that really stand out. Then, rank them in order of importance.

You might be able to fit only three or four events into the song, but your list should provide plenty of story choices.

## Verse vs. Chorus

There's a secret to storytelling in songs to maximize audience engagement. Much like all those Greek tragedies you were forced to read in high school (which was the real tragedy!), there's a key to ordering your song's story:

- Verse = events
- Chorus = emotions

The verses are perfect for telling your listeners about the story's events, and the repeating choruses should introduce the emotions—your feelings about the events. Each verse should help carry the story along until you reach the fantastic end, after which you sing the chorus one more time, revealing your overall emotions.

## Sing Your Story

Yes, singing your story is exactly what a storytelling songwriter does, but coming up with a catchy melody is one of the most challenging parts of the process. You may want to find a killer chorus or chord progression, but it's helpful to first sing the words to your story. It's like when your mom made you do your homework before you were allowed to go outside and have fun. Work first, play later.

Stories almost always have a cadence and rhythm of their own, helping you find the melody hidden inside. For example, instead of reading "The Great Gatsby," sing it. This will help you find the emphasis you want to put on certain parts of the song, and it'll help you find the right melody that flows naturally from the words.

**Learn Storytelling Structure**

Since you're writing a story into your song, it's vital to understand the basic storytelling structure. It's worked for countless authors in the past, and it'll work for you, too.

Throughout most of literary history, the primary storytelling structure has been this:

- Exposition
- Rising Action
- Climax
- Falling Action
- Resolution

Since most songs don't have five verses (unless you're Don McLean writing "American Pie"), you might have to combine a few parts into a single verse.

You're also welcome to cut some parts if you wish, but most songs should follow a basic arc structure: intro, rising action, climax, and resolution. Build the emotions up and resolve them at the end.

While following such a tried-and-true structure is always considered a good idea ...

## Break the Rules

FYI - the songwriting police aren't going to lock you away if you don't follow the "rules." Creativity has no rules.

If you think of an idea, follow it, regardless of whether it follows the norm. Many songs are great _because_ they're different, so don't be afraid to pursue your own path to telling stories through music.

## Be Open to Collaboration

Collaborating with a partner is a great way to improve your already-stellar stories. It's not always easy to develop story ideas, but no one said you had to do it alone. The right partner can make all the difference in the world.

You can collaborate on various aspects of the songwriting process. Work with someone to help flesh out a solid story, build a compelling melody, or edit the narrative to ensure it's as powerful as possible. You often get superior results working together than either of you could have produced alone. The whole is greater than the sum of its parts.

## Beg, Borrow, and (Don't) Steal

Want to know a secret about writing songs about stories? The stories don't always have to be yours or even true. There are these large buildings called libraries that are separated into fiction and non-fiction. It's a great resource for stories.

Whether using something you saw on the news, read in a book, or even stumbled upon in a social media post, inspiration is everywhere. You just have to look for it.

Not only is "borrowing" a story a great way to find inspiration, but it can help you connect with your audience over something shared. For example, if you reference Romeo and Juliet—as many, many songs have—most of your listeners are familiar with the story and can connect with it.

**Follow Your Own Process**

Although it might seem counterintuitive to this list, the main takeaway for anything songwriting related is to follow your own process. There's no secret formula that'll let you write great songs. Every writer has their own process for creating great content. You just need to take the time to find yours and be brave enough to follow it. That's the secret to great storytelling, songwriting, and living! [8]

"Be authentic. If, while writing, your thoughts bring your emotions to the surface, you're onto something. If you feel it deeply, chances are the rest of humanity will. Universal feelings matter most in songs," said Les Sampou, a singer-songwriter as well as a winner of the Lyrics category of the 2021 USA Songwriting Competition.

---

[8] (Brandon, Songwriting Secrets to Create Better Stories, 2022)

*Scott Ashley*

## Chapter 10:

# How to Write a Melody for Any Lyric

As if writing lyrics wasn't hard enough, now you have to add a melody to the words. After all, without a tune, lyrics are just a poem. If you struggle with creating an engaging tune to accompany your incredible words, here are a few tips to help you write a melody for any lyric.

**1. Read Your Lyrics Aloud**

Speaking has a natural cadence to it. In English, statements typically start high and end low, while questions usually finish on a high note.

One of the best ways to write a melody for your lyrics is to simply speak your lyrics aloud multiple times. You might be surprised how the natural cadence of your speech turns into a catchy melody. Try speaking at different tempos to find what sounds best.

It can be challenging to speak and hear a melody simultaneously, so make sure you have a voice recorder handy. You may have a voice-memo app on your cellphone. By recording yourself speaking the lyrics, you can replay the recording and maybe catch a hidden melody you didn't hear while you were speaking.

## 2. Find the Climax

A tune or melody is supposed to support the lyrics and can't be thrown haphazardly into your song. The lyrics are designed to convey emotion, and so should your melody.

To create a melody that supports your lyrics, rank the emotionalism of your lyrics on a scale of 1 to 10. Under each line, write how strong you think the lyric is emotionally. If it's a super emotional, amazing line, give it a 10. If it's just a supporting line, it may only be worth a 1 or 2.

Jumps in melodies bring out the emotions. The bigger the jump, the more the feeling. A big jump means big feelings. Think of Whitney Houston singing "I Will Always Love You."

Once you rank your lyrics, just follow along with the numbers under the lines to build your melody. This will help your melody line follow the emotionalism of your lyrics—and make your song more engaging. Remember, big numbers (emotional) mean bigger jumps between notes.

## 3. Use Your Instrument

Sometimes it helps to get some melodic inspiration from an outside source. Grab your favorite instrument for making chords—typically a guitar or piano—and play the first chord of your song. Then, sing the tonic note. If you play a G chord, sing a G note.

Start singing your lyrics on that note and experiment with some rhythms. Hold certain notes longer if they deserve more feeling (see the previous tip about ranking the lines on an emotional scale).

This suggestion might not help you write the entire melody for your song. Still, it'll help your brain transition from thinking of your lyrics as just words on a page and more like lyrics to a song.

Repeat the process, adding a few more chords, and see what melodies and rhythms you come up with.

**4. Get Into It!**

Songwriting is all about feeling. When you think about it, it's basically just dramatic speaking. If you want to write a great melody, get into it and act it out!

If you want to write a sad melody, get low. Writing a heavy rock song? Stomp your feet, clench your fists, get angry, and roar! If you want to write a happy tune, be bubbly.

Don't be afraid to overact while reciting your lyrics. If professional wrestlers can get away with it, so can you. You'll develop an emotional melody that fits your lyrics in no time.

**5. Add Some Rhythm**

If you're still struggling to come up with a good melody, it helps to add a little context. Give yourself some rhythm to work with by using a backing track or even starting a metronome to just provide a steady rhythmic beat. Speaking or singing with a metronome will also help you decide if you should go faster or slower.

Hearing the rhythm underneath your lyrics can help you develop some new and creative melodies. At the very least, you might get some rhythm ideas to use after you come up with the perfect melody.

## 6. Listen to Other Artists

Music doesn't exist in a vacuum. Listening to other artists is a great way to find inspiration for your melodies.

Actively listen to other artists, paying close attention to how they have constructed their melodies and phrasing as the tune relates to the lyrics. If you notice they always seem to swell at moving or emotional parts, consider incorporating that concept into your writing.

We're not suggesting you should copy other artists' melodies. We've already mentioned that and how some artists have gotten into serious trouble for incorporating too much from other songs. Use _general_ ideas, not specific phrasing. Make sure your creation is still all yours.

## 7. Build Your Perfect Melody

You already have the lyrics; now you need the perfect melody. Luckily, your lyrics can help you write the tune for your song. Read your words aloud, follow the emotions, use your instrument, act it out, use some backing rhythm, and listen to other artists for inspiration. You'll have that perfect melody in no time, and your listeners will be humming along.

Don't be discouraged if it takes longer to write the lyrics than the melody. Some songwriters spend a much more significant portion of time writing the lyrics.

Read what Diane Warren had to say on the subject in an NPR interview from 2010:

"Lyrics are what take the most time," said Diane Warren, a legendary multi-hit songwriter with #1 hits on the Billboard Hot 100 charts, including "Nothing's Gonna Stop Us Now" by Starship and "Because You Loved Me" by Céline Dion. The music usually comes to Warren quickly, but she's more careful with the lyrics, "to really make sure the idea is really developed and really compelling and great." She estimates she spends about a week on a song.[9]

---

[9] (NPR, 2010)

*Scott Ashley*

# Chapter 11:

# Toplining

**What is Toplining?**

Toplining is writing a vocal part over an existing music bed. This is popular in the EDM, Pop, R&B, and Hip-Hop/Rap world. It is a different sense of songwriting in that you <u>are</u> writing a crucial section of the song. However, it is also <u>not</u> songwriting because you're not creating a new song entirely from scratch.

If someone hires you to do toplining, they've already created the "beats" or music, and you're expected to write the melody and lyrics. They have recorded all the tracks except the "topline," the melody with lyrics.

**What skills do you need as a Topline Songwriter?**

If you're a topliner, your musical gifts should include your ability to:

- write catchy melodies
- add good lyrics, and
- sing well

## Legal Case Involving Toplining

In 2011, there was a famous legal case involving DJ Avicii versus Leona Lewis to settle a dispute in which the Swedish DJ attempted to get a high court injunction to block the release of Lewis's new single, "Collide." The suit alleged that the instrumental track for the single was copied from Avicii's forthcoming single, "Fade Into Darkness."

How did Leona Lewis end up recording an almost identical track to Avicii's without realizing their releases were going to collide?

The dispute arose due to a common practice – especially among DJ/producers and dance labels such as Avicii's label, Ministry of Sound. A track is sent to a plethora of topline writers to create melody and lyrics demos (the topline) for the track. The writers record their topline, and the DJ selects the one they like the best. In this specific case, one of the topline demos that was not picked—but contained Avicii's *backing track*—found its way to Lewis. She recorded it, prompting the dispute.

## Why do people hire topliners?

Producers are often very talented at creating beats and synth tracks. They can do this part but aren't confident in their melody or lyric writing skills. That's where a topliner comes in. Other times, instrument players want to hire topliners instead of writing a whole song themselves. There are many legitimate reasons to hire topliners. It's very similar to collaborating with other creative individuals.

**How common is toplining?**

Many writers do it for EDM, Pop, R&B, and Hip-Hop/Rap producers, commercials, bands, and other situations where people don't want to write the vocal part. The other 10% is songwriting – writing the entire song for clients from the ground up. If you're going to get paid work as a songwriter, you'll definitely want to try toplining as an option.

**How do I get started as a topliner?**

First, you'll need to hone your craft. Don't take a paid gig until you know exactly how to do it. Get some free music beds or background music online and practice writing melodies and lyrics to it. See how many ideas you can create. Use one track to create several songs.

Another practical step is to set up your social media and let people know you're available for toplining services.

**How do I get paid for toplining?**

This part can be tricky since you are writing a portion of the song but not all of it. You can work this in several ways.

- Option 1: No up-front pay, but a larger royalty split

I actually don't recommend this one often. Unless you are sure the song will sell and generate revenue (if the client already has proven sales and a large following), you're unlikely to make a ton of money from royalties. Still, it might be an option if you want the work and the client doesn't have money but is willing to split 50/50 with you.

- Option 2: Work For Hire (no royalties, all upfront pay)

This is the most common scenario for many topline writers. Many do this because they are unsure what will happen to the song after they are done with it, and they need the money up front (*musicians don't often live lavishly, in case you're wondering*). However, the obvious downside is that if the song becomes huge, the topline writer will make nothing from sales – no royalties. Deciding if this is a risk you're willing to take is important.

- Option 3: A combination of the above

Let's say you are offered a lower rate than you would typically accept, or the client doesn't have enough to pay your usual fee. This is a good time to negotiate royalties with them if you're willing to do this. Create an amount of upfront pay combined with royalties to make both of you happy.

Toplining isn't for everyone. It is not taking the place of traditional songwriting. Both areas require similar skills, and there is a definite crossover, but it reflects today's new technological possibilities. Done well, toplining can produce catchy songs that are fun to listen to and fulfilling to write.[10]

---

[10] (Brandon, How to Become a Topline Songwriter, 2019)

*Scott Ashley*

# Chapter 12:

# Tips to Help You Complete a Song

Whether you're a beginner songwriter or a seasoned veteran, starting a song is always easy, but finishing it is a different story. You get a spark of inspiration for a catchy chorus or musical intro, but you can never find a good verse, hook, or melody that fits. The unfinished song languishes in your notebook (or on your iPhone or iPad) for all eternity.

To turn that piece of an idea into a fully-formed song, here are six tips to help you cross the finish line.

> *"I have a structured songwriting process. I start with the music and try to come up with musical ideas, then the melody, then the hook, and the lyrics come last. Some people start with the lyrics first because they know what they want to talk about and they just write a whole bunch of lyrical ideas, but for me, the music tells me what to talk about."*
>
> — John Legend, Grammy Award winner [11]

## 1. Set Small Goals

It's easy to get excited about a big goal like releasing an entire album. But if you try to sit down and write a whole album at

---

[11] (Ditto Music, 2018)

once, it quickly feels daunting or overwhelming, leading to a disappointing, unfinished project.

The old saying is still true: "How do you eat an elephant? One bite at a time." Set small, manageable goals to help you stay on course. Instead of attempting to write an entire album, write a chorus. The next day, write a verse or two, maybe a hook the day after, and so on. Putting a few small goals together will quickly produce a complete song without generating nearly as much stress.

## 2. Focus on Your Strengths

Why would you try to teach an eagle to swim when it flies so well already? You should use the same idea with your songwriting. If you're a killer lyricist, but your hooks and melodies are lacking, find a co-writer to put some chords behind your words and create a better lead line.

There are plenty of times in this life you are required to do things you don't care to do. This shouldn't be one of them. Focus on your strengths and either find someone to help you with the parts you're not good at or outsource them completely. Forcing yourself to do something you don't like is the quickest path to quitting.

You can see this idea in action in real life. Elton John is one of the most popular musicians of the last century, but he doesn't like writing lyrics. The lyrics to most of his hits, including "Candle in the Wind" and "Your Song," were written by his long-time writing partner, Bernie Taupin. Elton knows Bernie can write better lyrics, so he lets him! There's no rule against you doing the same thing.

Focus on what you're good at, and let someone else help with the other parts. Remove some of the frustrations of writing a song, and you're more likely to get to the finish line.

**3. Listen to the World Around You**

You might be temporarily pumped about that hook that just popped into your head, but if the lyrics or verses don't come just as quickly, you're more likely to give up on the idea. Many people give up writing a song because they lose their inspiration.

Listen to the world around you for inspiration to finish a song. Have you ever been walking down the street, heard a mechanical tone, and thought, "Is that a D?" You may have even found yourself building little melodies off the bass pedal tone of a lawnmower or some other piece of equipment.

Tell the truth: haven't you ever found yourself bobbing your head, tapping your fingers, and creating a beat to the clicking of your car's turn signal? Inspiration can be anywhere, including everyday noises we may not even notice anymore. We need to train ourselves to hear the world again.

Think about the Billy Joel song "Allentown," with its whooshes and clunks that mimic the sounds of a steel mill.

Music is all around us if we're willing to listen and recognize it. If you want an idea of how this works, check out a clip from the 2007 movie "August Rush," about an 11-year-old musical prodigy living in an orphanage who runs away to New York City. In the clip, August hears the music in all the sounds around him on the streets of New York. https://youtu.be/9hrDNGmAigU

**4. Have Your Recorder Ready**

Musical ideas can pop up at a moment's notice, so be ready. Always have a recorder or your smartphone handy to catch any glimpses of inspiration that might appear. You might think, "I don't need to record it; I'll remember," but how often do you actually remember after you get back to your workspace?

Keep your recorder nearby and have it ready to capture any idea or thought that might help you finish your song. You never know when inspiration will hit.

> *"For me, when I'm writing a song, I always have my phone or writing pad close by, I even take it to bed with me (sounds funny right?)," said Wilbur "B52" Levans, First Prize winner of the Hip-Hop category of the 2021 USA Songwriting Competition.*

In a Howard Stern show interview, hit Artist/Songwriter/Rapper Post Malone said that he writes most of his hit songs sitting on the toilet. (TMI?)

## 5. Know What It Takes to Turn an Idea into a Song

That little clip you recorded on your phone isn't a song—yet. But it is a good start. The key to finishing a composition is understanding what is required to turn an idea into a song.

To complete a song takes a few different parts: the chorus, verses, melody, bridge, hook, or even a funky breakdown. That clip on your phone might work for one of those parts, but remember that it doesn't count as a complete song.

Knowing what to do with all the pieces you collect is just as important as understanding your instrument of choice. It's easier to piece inspiration together if you can recognize the needed parts. Taking the time to first learn the fundamentals of songwriting will aid you in completing songs in the future.

## 6. Step Back and Take a Walk

Step back and take a minute to regroup if you can't think of what to add to your song. Remember, songwriting is supposed to be fun. Frustration isn't good for anything.

If you're stumped by writer's block and can't figure out how to get that awesome chord progression, don't throw down your notebook and give up—as tempting as that may be. Walk away, take a breath, and come back to it when your mind is fresh.

Frustration is the primary killer of songwriting. Unfortunately, it's something you're guaranteed to encounter. You're better equipped to finish your song if you know how to deal with the inevitable frustration.

"When writing songs, I usually begin with what inspires my creativity. I love to be spontaneous so I don't usually sit down with a plan in mind." So said Sonny King, First Prize winner of the R&B category in the 2021 USA Songwriting Competition. He continued, "There have been times I have been inspired by an artist's story or vibe and even felt inspiration from other artists' works, but generally I often start with a chord progression that gives me that certain feeling where I just know this could lead somewhere."

With these tips in mind, you're ready to get out there and actually finish your song. [12]

---

[12] (Brandon, 6 Tips to Help You Complete a Song, 2022)

## Chapter 13:

# Beatles Songwriting Secrets I Wish I Knew Earlier

John Lennon and Paul McCartney wrote twenty songs that hit #1 on the Billboard Hot 100 Charts. Though unclear for how much longer, the Beatles still reign supreme as the artist with the most #1 songs of all time. Many songwriters draw their inspiration from the Beatles. The second and third spots belong to artists not known for being songwriters: Elvis with eighteen chart-toppers and Mariah Carey with nineteen.

The Beatles accomplished the remarkable feat in only eight years. Sir Paul has continued to write since the Beatles' breakup, adding 19 more hits (with Wings and as a solo artist) on top of the twenty he wrote with John Lennon. Lennon's untimely murder in 1980 sundered any hopes of a future reunion by the songwriting duo.

Even more remarkable is that none of the band members had formal music education: they didn't read or write music. Even though they may not have known the correct terminology, they had a basic, raw understanding of music theory. They knew what typically went together and what sounded good. Perhaps most helpful to their writing was that they were unafraid to experiment, learning as they went.

Their producer, George Martin (often called the fifth Beatle), *did* have formal music training. He used his skills and training to translate the band's music into notation. This was invaluable when other musicians came in to play on their songs – string or horn players, for example. Martin also made numerous suggestions and contributed arrangements that strengthened the band's songlist.

The Beatles knew music intuitively, much like you can drive a car without knowing how to put one together. Working with George Martin and desiring to "do better" helped the Fab Four become better songwriters. Having even the most basic grasp of music theory can help you "look under the hood" of your favorite songs so you can understand them better and take your writing to a new level.

The Beatles (and many other bands) prove that not having a formal music education doesn't mean you can't write great music. Go with your ear and your gut, and follow your inspiration.

The songwriting partnership between Lennon and McCartney is legendary. The songwriting styles of John Lennon and Paul McCartney differed fundamentally and changed over time, affected and influenced by circumstances, each other, and their respective lives. They employed countless tricks anyone can borrow for their songwriting arsenal. Entire books are still being written that analyze the Beatles' songs, most delving deeply into the music theory of the songs.

Like John, Paul, George, and Ringo, most songwriters have an *instinctive* understanding of music, meaning they know what sounds good, works together, and sells. They may not know the difference between a flat Major Seventh chord and a diminished third, but like the Beatles, they love writing songs that make you stop and listen.

Here are some secrets and tricks of the Beatles.[13]

## 1. Change up your chorus

At a time when most songs began with an instrumental introduction followed by the first verse, the Beatles were starting some songs with the chorus. Some of their greatest hits open with a chorus hybrid that previews the title and hooks. This pattern shows up in their hit "She Loves You." Unusual at the time, the song erupts with the hook right away instead of introducing it after a verse or two. "She Loves You" does not include a bridge, using the refrain to join the various verses instead. The chords change every two measures, and the harmonic scheme is mostly stationary.

Another example of changing up the chorus is in the song "Help." The intro has the same chord progression as the

---

[13] (Brandon, 7 Beatles Secrets about Songwriting I wish I'd Discovered Decades Sooner (Part 2), 2018)

chorus, but it moves twice as fast and features the title four times as opposed to the chorus's three.[14]

Use this chorus trick, and the listener will be hooked by the reassuring feeling that they've heard your song somewhere before when you reach your chorus.

**2. Add Blues to Your Melody**

Before the Beatles made it big, they spent a lot of time playing covers of other artists' songs, which meant a lot of Rhythm & Blues. R&B was raw and edgy, parents hated it, and kids loved it, which is part of the reason for its popularity—to make mom and dad crazy.

Through playing and singing R&B, it became a natural, comfortable part of their makeup. Bluesing up a song was just part of who they were – flattening a note to give it more soul. A single note or two in your melody can make the song more relatable, even emotional. Blues notes are akin to crying in your song. It's as though you go from telling the story to reliving the pain, which comes out in the notes.

Adding blues notes can be tricky to pull off if you're not a confident singer — you might not want to insert the blues note into your chord until you've learned to pitch it correctly. Using blues notes adds a soulful edge to your melodies.

---

[14] (Blick, 2012)

## 3. Delay the Root Chord

Starting a song on the tonic chord (like playing a C chord for a song in the key of C) is a rut the Beatles managed to avoid a surprising number of times.

"Eleanor Rigby" is a perfect example of delaying the root chord. The song starts on C major before heading to the home chord – e minor. It's one of the many things that gives the track an immediate sense of tension. Using this trick will give your progressions more forward momentum. [15]

## 4. Utilize The Outside Chord & Use non-diatonic chords and secondary dominants [16]

Many of us employ 'out of key' chords, whether we realize it or not. Out of 186 Beatles compositions, only 22 remained solidly in key.

In "Strawberry Fields Forever," Lennon pulls the rug out from under the Bb major tonality by replacing the F major chord you expect with an F minor.

(Bb) Let me take you down 'cos I'm going to… (Fm)

It's like the stomach drop you experience as you go over the crest of a rollercoaster. Later, Lennon creates a

---

[15] (Blick, 2012)
[16] (Blick, 2012)

disorientating momentary high by replacing the Gm with a G major.

(Eb) Nothing to get (G) hung about

The introduction for "Strawberry Fields Forever" is played on a Mellotron, and the vocals enter with the chorus instead of a verse. In fact, we are not "taken down" to the tonic key but to "non-diatonic chords and secondary dominants" combined with "chromatic melodic tension intensified through outrageous harmonization and root movement."

Outside chords will surprise your listeners and freshen your melodies.

## 5. Restate Your Lyrics

Lennon's lyrics to "A Day in the Life" were inspired by then-current newspaper articles, including a report on the death of Guinness heir Tara Browne.

John Lennon wrote the melody and most of the lyrics to the verses of "A Day in the Life" in mid-January 1967. Soon after, he presented the song to Paul McCartney, who contributed a middle-eight section.

The Beatles didn't make their lyrics memorable by simply repeating sections wholesale. They also repeated and adapted words, phrases, and sentence structures.[17] "A Day

---

[17] (Blick, 2012)

In The Life" is comprised of four verses, a middle eight section, and only one repeated line.

And yet it's memorable (in part) because of lyrical verse links like these:

*I read the news/saw a film today, oh boy*
*and though the news was rather sad/holes were rather small*
*found my way downstairs/coat/way upstairs*
*I just had to laugh/look*

This subtle trick will make your lyrics "sticky" and give a sense of unity to a track.

## 6. Take Risks

In many ways, "Here There and Everywhere" is the opposite of "Eleanor Rigby" in that, harmonically speaking, it is rich and complex.

The introduction, "To lead a better life," opens in the key of G and involves a G-Bm-Bb-Am7-D7 chord progression. The Bb chord on "I need my love to be here" is a dissonant substitute for the more predictable E7 that would typically lead to the Am chord.[18]

This marks the first time Paul really spreads his compositional wings and takes some larger risks with an ascending major chord sequence. The song walks up and down the scale repeatedly. The main verse progression is a

---

[18] (Blick, 2012)

walk-up that is now standard for many (post-Beatles) songs: G-Am-Bm-C-G.

## 7. Change of Keys from Minor to Major

"While My Guitar Gently Weeps," initially issued by the Beatles in the key of A minor, changes to A major over the bridges. Aside from the intro, the composition is structured into two rounds of verse and bridge, with an instrumental passage extending the second of these verse sections, followed by a final verse and a lengthy instrumental passage that fades out on the recording. All the sections consist of an even sixteen bars or measures, each divided into four phrases.

The change to the parallel major key is heralded by a C chord as the verse's penultimate chord (replacing the D used in the second phrase of each verse) before the E that leads into the bridge.

Musicologist Alan Pollack views this combination of C and E as representing a sense of "arrival," after which the bridge contains "upward [harmonic] gestures" that contrast with the bass descents that dominate the verse.[19] Such contrasts are limited by the inclusion of minor triads (III, VI, and II) played over the E chord that ends the bridge's second and fourth phrases.[20]

---

[19] (Pollack, 2001)
[20] (Blick, 2012)

The change from a minor to a major key is built up perhaps most dramatically and satisfactorily in "A Day in the Life" from the Sgt. Pepper album. The instruments walk up in a seemingly semi-organized fashion but become overlaid with dissonance and noise until the listener finally bursts out at the top – in the major key. You have a genuine sense of arrival when you reach the culmination of the mode change.

*"I don't work at being ordinary" ~ Paul McCartney*

*Scott Ashley*

# Chapter 14:

# Tips for Entering Songwriting Competitions

Most people think Songwriting Competitions have to be a pain-inducing experience on par with getting a root canal. The truth is that for many songs that have done well, the writers took steps to ensure they sound good. As you read through these ten tips on entering songwriting competitions, you'll discover it doesn't have to be a long, complicated process. You probably already have all the knowledge necessary to write a great song.

Entering Songwriting Competitions can reveal how good your songs really are. The following ten tips will help you improve your chances of doing well in Songwriting Competitions.

**1. Vocals & Pronunciation**

Put the vocals high in the mix, make sure the vocalist pronounces the lyrics correctly, and the pronunciation is clear. Lyrics that can't be heard can't be judged. If people unfamiliar with your song can't follow the story, you need to remix it, so your poignant lyrics aren't overpowered by the band.

Our event director, Eddie Phoon, was a panelist on a demo listening panel at a Nashville Music Conference several years ago. The panel consisted of A&R directors from record labels and music publishing companies. They listened to a Rock/Alternative song, and all the panelists liked it except Eddie. He said he liked the song but not the lyrics. He said he didn't understand the lyrics, "Open Your Ass." The band responded, "No, it's open your EARS," and the crowd roared with laughter! Lesson learned: enunciate your lyrics to ensure the listener knows what you are singing about.

## 2. Make Sure Your Song Is in the Right Category

Just because you sing about Nashville doesn't make it a country song. If you don't sound like Carrie Underwood or Eric Church, hire someone who does to sing your song. Add some weepy pedal steel and a mournful fiddle, and make sure there's a little twang in the singer's voice if country is your goal.

Is it jazz? It should have something beyond a single ninth chord and a host of major chords. Use chord substitutions to give it that smooth jazz sound. Is it folk? Add an acoustic guitar. Bluegrass? Better put in a banjo.

Lyrics are important, too. If you're singing about trucks and bars, it's not jazz unless you've been at the aforementioned bar and consumed a couple of whiskeys on the rocks.

It should go _without_ saying, but it needs to be said: listen to songs popular in your writing style and note their lyrics and arrangements. Don't be the songwriter who wastes a good song by submitting it in the wrong category.

## 3. Arrangement & Collaboration

A Songwriting Competition is not an arrangement contest. We don't care if Clapton is your guitar player. Give us a compelling story or lyrics rich in metaphor. Try a Best Band contest if you want to show off your hotshot guitar player. Instrumentals are in a separate category. For those, make sure there's an engaging melody repeated several times.

If you feel proficient at writing song melodies but weak at lyrics, find a lyric writer and collaborate with them. In the past five years of the USA Songwriting Competition, all top winning songs were collaborations. The same holds true for the Top 40 hits on the Billboard Hot 100 Charts; most of today's hits are collaborations.

## 4. Keep the Intro Short. No, Even Shorter.

The judges have already listened to a hundred songs, and each consumed a pot of coffee. They don't need a 24-bar intro. Everyone knows "Stairway to Heaven" has a really long cool introduction, but you are not Led Zeppelin. Be kind to your judges.

Get to the lyrics in eight bars or less. If it's an instrumental, get to the central melody right away.

**5. Have an Accurate Lyric Sheet**

If your lyric sheet has a word or two that's different, it's not a problem, but make sure all the verses are included and everything else fundamental to the song. A missing bridge, especially one with the song's theme, could cost you the coveted prize, and if you forget the last verse, we'll never know if mama gets out of prison.

**6. Avoid Overused Rhymes**

Skip rhymes like heart/start, fire/desire, shelf/self, do/blue, together/weather, right/light, and light/night. They are clichés. "You are my fire, my one desire...." They've been used in thousands of songs and have completely lost their emotional impact.

A good rhyming dictionary can be invaluable. Don't forget imperfect rhymes – the ones where the vowel sound matches but maybe not much else, such as right/fly or cape/lane.

**7. Don't Use Rain as a Metaphor for Sadness**

Fred Rose already wrote "Blue Eyes Crying in the Rain," and Willie Nelson sang it. You can't top that. Likewise, don't use storms as a metaphor for anger or sunny days for being happy. Even better: stay away from weather metaphors. Songs like that have been done before. Try to write in a refreshing manner.

## 8. Tune Your Guitar

Many judges are musicians themselves, and unlike some audience members, they not only notice an out-of-tune guitar but are also distracted by it. It demands their complete attention. Likewise, a drummer that's always a half-beat off or harmonies that are sour will draw the judges' focus, and those are not things you want to attract their focus.

True, it's *not* a Best Band contest, but why complicate matters? It's difficult for the judges to hear a melody sung off-key, yet many song demos are off-key.

## 9. Don't Tell Us Your Emotions; Show Us

"I'm sad you left me" is boring. Tell us about the rose you found pressed in the family Bible or finding his keys on the kitchen counter. Think like a good cinematographer. A talking head is coma-inducing ("I feel sad" or "You're so mean"), but add a vivid landscape and a great mystery, and you've got Citizen Kane. In other words: show, don't tell.

## 10. Look for a Unique Angle with Detail

"She broke my heart and left me" has been sung a million times. Seriously. We don't care anymore. "She slammed the door on the way out and ran over my foot with her new cherry red Ford truck" – that's more interesting because it has details and tells an old story in a new way.

Use all your senses. Did he give you a rose? How did it smell? Don't just tell us it's red – go to a thesaurus and tell us it's fuchsia, deep pink, or maroon. Don't tell us you like his kiss. Tell us how it tastes. Don't tell us her dress is pretty; tell us it feels like warm silk.

Too often, songs submitted to the USA Songwriting Competition sound like they were cranked out of a photocopier. Songwriters try to write a song that sounds like a current chart topper. It just ends up being awkward. Many songs we hear are derivative in their melodic lines and contain lyrics we feel may have been plagiarized.

One case was a songwriter who took the entire track of Jennifer Lopez's song "If You Had My Love" and wrote a "new" melody with the background music, but even the melodic line's rhythm was just like the original. The chorus was almost an exact copy of the original melody. The judges felt the song was plagiarized and unoriginal. The icing on the cake was when the judges left the room singing the Jennifer Lopez song, not the song that had been entered. Not surprisingly, that song didn't win.

Now, tune your guitar, find a drummer who can keep a steady beat, some singers with ears, and write some great songs.[21]

---

[21] (Brandon, Top Ten tips for Entering Songwriting Competitions, 2018)

## Chapter 15:

## Collaborations & Focusing On Your Strengths

Do you need help writing your song? This book mentions collaborating with another person or persons several times. Collaborations can be very fruitful. Writing songs with someone else can help you through the weak spots of your songs and produce something fresh, new, and solid.

One of the top ten questions industry newcomers asked the late songwriter Ralph Murphy was, "How do I get heard in the music business?" Before he could answer that, he needed to know exactly what it was they wanted "heard." Ralph typically asked them about their goals – whether they wanted to be songwriters or recording artists – and the most frequent response was, "Both."

"The unfortunate truth is that, while many of the newcomers I counsel may be gifted as songwriters or singers, very few are equally blessed with both talents. While one ability may come rather naturally, the other often needs significant honing," Ralph Murphy said. Murphy wrote songs such as "Half the Way" by Crystal Gayle.[22]

---

[22] (Murphy, 2017)

*"If you spend too much time working on your weaknesses, all you end up with is a lot of strong weaknesses."* — *Dan Sullivan, Business trainer*

## Listen to the truth

Murphy said, "the unfortunate truth is that, while many of the newcomers I counsel may be gifted as songwriters or singers, very few are equally blessed with both talents. While one ability may come rather naturally, the other often needs significant honing."

Murphy continued, "the problem is, not everyone wants to hear the truth. Some great singers (who are average songwriters) can make the really average songs they've written shine through the sheer power of their vocal ability. They make the phrase 'I love you' sound so good that you almost believe they invented it.

In equal numbers come the great songwriters (who are average singers) who have been told by family, friends, lovers, and late-night adoring coffeehouse/honky-tonk buffoons that, despite the fact that their tempo, pitch, and teeth are bad, they have star quality. And no matter how badly they sing, their songs are strong enough to survive a mediocre vocal performance and sound like hits." [23]

---

[23] (Murphy, 2017)

## Check your ego at the door

"The bottom line," Murphy said, "is losing your ego. It's called 'absenting of self.' The person most likely to come between you and your career goal is you. Don't make the best of your talent a donkey for the least of your talent. Get some unbiased feedback from industry pros, available through various NSAI programs (Nashville Songwriters Association International). If you are weaker in one area, focus on your strength."[24]

Melissa Axel is an Artist Relations representative of the USA Songwriting Competition. She has been writing songs since she was eight years old. The piano-driven singer/songwriter studied at Boston's renowned Berklee College of Music and went on to earn her master's degree in Interdisciplinary Arts from Nova Southeastern University.

Melissa says, "many of us have grown accustomed to making music alone in our creative caves and may be nervous about teaming up with other writers. Let's look at some benefits of creative collaboration, whether in the same room or online with a co-writer many miles away." [25] The following tips are from Melissa.

---

[24] (Murphy, 2017)
[25] (Axel, 2011)

## Different minds bring fresh perspectives

Unless you've been deliberately writing about various subjects, your songs likely tend to focus on the handful of topics you know best or care about most. Pairing with someone else brings a new lifetime of experiences to the writing table. You'll see what another person's ideas look like when told through your eyes.

## Variation opens up new melodic and harmonic possibilities

If you tend to favor the same keys and chord progressions, writing with someone whose first instrument is different from yours can lead you down fresh musical paths. Guitarists can try writing with a pianist, violinist, cellist, mandolin player, etc. (and vice versa). Look for people who share some of your influences and lyrical interests but are into other musical styles or approaches to songwriting. Find an artist or writer comfortable in a territory that's new to you, and give it a try.

Example: Johnny Cash covering the song "Hurt" by Nine Inch Nails in 2002.

## Two heads really are better than one

It's easy to beat our heads against the wall or put a song aside for years when we're stuck on a section of lyrics or a melody that just doesn't feel "right." You may have some choruses that need verses or a song missing a bridge. Trusted writing partners can bounce ideas off each other and even complete unfinished songs, making sure each word and note is the strongest possible choice.

**Where do you find people to co-write with?**

Be open to meeting songwriting partners if you travel to perform or attend songwriting conferences. Some may be performing artists in your local music community, others writers you know from songwriting websites and social network groups, composers who usually write instrumental music, or producers who create tracks for artists who only sing or rap. It's easy to write across the miles with apps like Zoom and Facetime or by sending MP3s and lyrics back and forth via email.

If you're ready to broaden your songwriting horizons, take your time and get to know potential co-writers and their writing styles. As your songwriting becomes more plentiful, diverse, and enriching, you'll be glad you reached out and found creative collaborators who are a really great fit.[26]

---

[26] (Axel, 2011)

*Scott Ashley*

# Chapter 16:

# Sad Truths Why Some Songwriters Never Succeed

It doesn't matter where you are in your songwriting career as long as you are serious about songwriting. You can be a well-established songwriting pro with gigs for major artists who know your revenues should be higher, or you can be a beginning songwriter trying to make your way. Regardless of your experience, you can achieve greater success.

Unfortunately, there are three "sad truths" why most independent songwriters will never succeed.

**Truth #1: The Most Successful Songwriters Tend to Get Paid More for Who They <u>Are</u> than What They <u>Do</u>.**

More than any other active songwriter today, Max Martin consistently places songs with today's most prominent music artists. Why? Because Max Martin has written and co-written 25 Billboard Hot 100 number-one hits, most of which he produced or co-produced. Five songs he wrote or co-wrote debuted at number one on the Hot 100, including "Can't Stop the Feeling" by Justin Timberlake and "Shake It Off" by Taylor Swift.

Max's songwriting credits put him in third place for most number-one singles on the chart, just behind Paul

McCartney with 32 and John Lennon with 26. Having also produced 25 number-one chart singles ties Max with The Beatles producer, George Martin (no relation).

First, some tough love. A law degree, a doctorate, multiple certifications, and 25 years of experience does not automatically equate with higher pay. You are not *entitled* to a high income.

The list of the highest-paid pro athletes in any sport changes almost daily. Their fortunes can turn on a dime – or an ankle! NBA player Derrick Rose was one of the highest-paid athletes at one point in his career, despite being riddled with injuries most of his career. His contract extension in 2021 for $ 43 million doesn't even get him into the top 30 for 2022-23, where the least of the best is expected to receive over $31 million for one season.

Tim Tebow, a Heisman Trophy winner as a college sophomore, was never able to find traction in the NFL. But he made millions in endorsements simply for being "Tim Tebow."

Politicians consistently pull in millions of dollars for book deals and speaking tours regardless of how good or bad they were in office because they have name recognition.

Building up who you are – establishing a recognizable name – is considerably more important (unfortunately) than what you do or your competency level. Getting into a party may depend on who you know, but getting often depends on who knows you.

**Truth #2: Never Attempting to Collaborate With Other Songwriters or Producers; Only Writing Songs On Your Own.**

When a songwriter refuses to collaborate with another writer or producer, it's seen as refusing to improve. All the finalist songs in the Pop and Country categories in the 2016 USA Songwriting Competition were collaborations written by two or more songwriters. This trend seems to be the same for most songs in the Top 40 of Billboard's Hot 100 Charts.

Getting an outside perspective on your song from a fellow musician can help bring out the best in your music. Everyone suffers from writer's block at some point, but collaborating with other musicians offers a great way to break new ground and get a fresh perspective on your song. Show them what you've got so far, discuss new ideas they suggest, and see what comes out of it. Two heads are usually better than one.[27]

TIP: You'll notice rap artists do this a lot. If you're an aspiring rapper or in the process of becoming a rap artist, make sure you take advantage of as many collaboration opportunities as possible.

---

[27] (Ditto Music, 2018)

## Scott Ashley

*"I like collaboration because, first of all, I'm good at writing lyrics. I don't know how to make beats. I don't play instruments. I'm not a good singer. So even when you see a solo album of mine, it's still a collaboration."*
— *Talib Kweli*

Remember to ask for feedback. It's easy to lose sight of whether your song is good or bad after you've spent hours and hours working, changing, and creating it yourself. So find someone you trust to give honest advice and whose opinion you value, and ask them to critique it. You might find they have fantastic insights into how it could be improved. Find someone who is not afraid to hurt your feelings – you want honest opinions.

*"I enjoy the collaboration. I always envied people who got to have that interaction. It's a nice change helping other people with their music and not being all about what I'm trying to do myself." — Beck* [28]

Elton John recognizes that his strength lies in writing music, particularly melodic lines, and his songwriting partner, Bernie Taupin, focuses on his strength – writing lyrics. Learn from the pros: If you are proficient in writing music but weak at lyrics, collaborate with a lyricist or a songwriter who is better at writing lyrics.

---

[28] (Ditto Music, 2018)

## Truth #3: Doing The Same Things Repeatedly and Hoping for Different Results.

Albert Einstein is broadly credited with saying, "insanity is doing the same thing over and over again, but expecting different results." Songwriters do that when they re-use the same chord progression and rhyming clichés and wonder why their songwriting doesn't improve.

You need to be willing to look for and accept a different approach—even a different concept of yourself and your music, musicianship, or songwriting. That may include a fundamental change in how you think of yourself, your role, songwriting, music artistry, and how you present yourself to the music industry or audience.

It might feel uncomfortable. It certainly will be different from what you see others doing in your same profession and music category.

Collaborations are one way you can fundamentally improve your songs. But most songwriters invest all their energy in only one means of increasing their value: trying to write better songs alone.

This is like trying to lose weight, keep it off, and become healthier by diet alone with no changes in the practices that caused the weight problem. You can indeed lose weight by focusing on a single and taking it to extremes, but any dieter will attest that you eventually hit a wall. There comes the point when no more weight comes off, even if you eat nothing but a lettuce leaf with a squirt of lemon for dinner each night.

Trying to get better and better and better at your "thing" will slam you into an income barrier and never lift you over that wall. You must improve your songwriting or music artistry to increase your value to your audience and the music industry. That means interacting with other songwriters.

You must improve yourself for more success, using a more sophisticated approach to your songwriting and musical artistry. Focus on learning the strategies proven to catapult to your music success.[29]

You can't improve your songwriting by sheer willpower. Come out of your room, into the sunshine, and play with others.

*(By the way: as it turns out, insanity might be crediting that insanity quote to Einstein repeatedly. He never said it.—ed.)*

---

[29] (Randle, 3 Uncomfortable Truths About Why Most Songwriters Never Crack Through To Success, 2017)

## Chapter 17:

# Four Types of Music Publishing Royalties

There are several ways to make money with your music. Unfortunately, it's never as simple as receiving a weekly paycheck from punching a time clock (but not nearly as mind-numbing). Music revenue is generated by royalties, which occur when a company or individual pays you to use your copyrighted works—your music. In other words, when someone plays your music, you get a cut.

There are four different types of royalties involved in music publishing:

- Mechanical royalties
- Performance royalties
- Synch royalties
- Print music royalties

One of the biggest mysteries and struggles of the music industry is how to get paid music royalties in the United States. If you really want to make money in the music industry, it's essential to understand the differences between the types of royalties and how they work. We often hear the cliché about the starving artist, but what about the artist who eats? How do musicians at the top of their game reap what they have sown? Here's your guide to the four types of royalties in music publishing.

*(NOTE: The area of songwriting royalties is a landscape of constant change, largely due to changes in technology. Information in this chapter may become outdated at any time. Interested individuals should be prepared to do personal research on this subject. The following information comprises an overview and is in no way exhaustive. —ed)*

**1. Mechanical Royalties**

Think back to the days of records and cassettes. Whenever music was produced, it required a "mechanical" process to reproduce it. Mechanical royalties are paid out whenever a copy of a song is made.

Of course, times have changed, and almost nothing is mechanical or analog anymore. Most modern mechanical royalties come from streaming services like Spotify, Pandora, Apple Music, and others, but only when a listener plays your song *on-demand* or *downloads* it. When your song plays over a streaming radio service, it's a different type of royalty. We'll come to that shortly.

Mechanical royalty rates are set by the U.S. Copyright Act. Most of the time, rates land around $0.06 per 100 on-demand streams. So, if someone listens to your song 100 times on Spotify, you'll get $0.06. It doesn't sound like much, but if you get into the thousands or millions of streams, that money can add up. If your listeners play your song 1.666 million times, you'll earn $1,000 in mechanical royalties.

In the United States, mechanical royalties are collected and distributed by the Harry Fox Agency and the Mechanical Licensing Collective (MLC). Music publishing companies like **Songtrust** and **Cdbaby** also collect Mechanical royalties.

## 2. Performance Royalties

In some instances, replaying your copyrighted songs aren't considered reproductions; they're performances. This is typically when your songs are played in public places, such as:

- On the radio
- In a bar or restaurant
- Radio services like Spotify or Pandora (not for on-demand streaming or downloads)

To start earning performance royalties, you'll need to register your song with a Performance Rights Organization (PRO) like **BMI**, **ASCAP**, **SESAC**, **SOCAN** (Canada), or **PRS** (UK). They'll then split the royalty between songwriter royalties and publishing royalties. You'll get the songwriter royalties, while your publishing company (if you work with one) will get the publishing royalties.

## 3. Synchronization (Sync) Royalties

Music always makes videos, movies, and games better. But like any other reproduction of copyrighted work, it costs money. When someone "synchs" your music to a visual media, you'll get paid synch royalties.

Like nearly everything connected to the internet, change is measured not in days or hours but minutes. In 2022, there are more licensing companies than you can count on five hands. And it feels like there's at least one new platform popping up every month.

"In the highly digitized world that we live in today, licensing music has become much easier for artists than ever before. Music licensing used to involve a lengthy process that required reaching out to many different stakeholders that had a say in who could license each piece of music. Now, artists can use a variety of digital platforms that make licensing your music for sync (TV, Film, Video Games, Ads, etc.) as easy as clicking a couple of buttons." [30]

Synchronization royalties are typically one-time fees. Synch licenses give the license holder the right to use copyrighted music in films, television, commercials, video games, online streaming, advertisements, and any other type of visual media. Sync licenses are generally sold by Music Publishers.

---

[30] (Brown, 2022)

Another note, a synchronization license does not include the right to use an existing recording with audiovisual media. That's right, if you want to use your favorite artist's version of a song, the licensee will also need to purchase a master use license before using copyrighted music with a new audiovisual project. So unless your plan was to re-record a brand-new version of the song you just licensed, you will have to contact the appropriate record label to purchase a Master Use License in addition to the sync license. Again, this goes for any audiovisual media—even YouTube.[31]

When a company decides to use your song in a commercial, they'll pay the royalties once, covering the life of the commercial. Once the song is synched, it's forever authorized for use in that particular visual media.

- Criteria To Consider

Before choosing which sync licensing libraries you want to work with, there are some criteria that you should consider in order to determine your best option.

- Quality of Music

The quality of music is arguably the most important thing that you should consider before choosing a platform. Bad music is an easy way to ruin any kind of video that you are

---

[31] (Indie Music Academy, 2022)

producing. For that reason, the quality should take the front seat in any of your considerations.

- User Interface

A well-thought-out user interface will ultimately make it easier for you to sign up, browse the platform, and license music for your project. The more time you spend browsing through music for your project, the less time you will have on the actual project. Choose a platform that allows you to narrow down your choices easily and efficiently.

- Cost

The cost of any licensing platform is important, especially if your project is on a tight budget. How much money you have to spend will depend on your specific needs for music. Do you need to license one song for a quick intro, or will you have needs for different tracks over time? First figure out what you actually need from a licensing platform and then you will have a better idea about how much money you need to spend.[32]

For a list of Licensing Companies, check out https://www.omarimc.com/best-music-sync-licensing-companies/

Don't let the songs you've written sit there and collect dust when they could be collecting royalties. With any of these

---

[32] (Brown, 2022)

easy-to-use sync licensing platforms mentioned above, you could easily be on your way to licensing and selling your own music.

## 4. Print Music Royalties

Whenever you wander through a music store, you'll probably see entire walls of print music and tabs to teach musicians how to play popular songs. Since printed music is different than audio reproductions or productions of a song, they need a different type of royalty.

Print music royalties are just like they sound: royalties that come from the sale of sheet (printed) music. These royalties are typically split between the songwriters and the publishers. Naturally, this type of royalty applies only to songwriters who release their songs as sheet music. By focusing only on mechanical and performance royalties, it's common for musicians to not receive any print music royalties.

Obviously, most music is digital these days. To learn how to play a particular song, most people today search Google or YouTube. Print music royalties are typically small compared to other music revenue streams. However, they still exist—especially for composers and musicians who create full-ensemble or concert music. There are also digital print rights for eBooks, digital sheet music, etc. Full-ensemble, concert, and sacred (church) sheet music is seeing a resurgence through printable digital downloads.

## Get Paid for Your Music

Getting paid for your music might not be as simple or straightforward as getting a paycheck from an employer. Still, there are several avenues for bringing in revenue. When you release a new song, make sure you get the most for your work by understanding which of the four types of royalties apply to you. Between mechanical royalties, performance royalties, synch royalties, and print music royalties, it's possible to make a decent living as a musician.

If you're unsure about which types of royalties you're entitled to, it's a good idea to speak to an attorney. Determining what applies to your situation and which steps to take can be complicated. You worked hard to create your music and deserve to be paid. Get the royalties you've earned. [33]

---

[33] (Brandon, 4 Types of Royalties Involved in Music Publishing, 2022)

# Chapter 18:

# Copyright Your Songs

While many creatives in the entertainment industry believe (and are partly correct) that a work is copyrighted as soon as it is fixed in a tangible medium it still pays, often literally, to formally register the work with the U.S. Copyright Office (USCO), particularly where legal issues are concerned.

The USCO website is at: https://www.copyright.gov/

First: do you need to copyright your music? Contrary to belief, music copyright isn't as complex as you might've been led to believe.

However (while the technicalities vary from country to country) the basic principle remains the same – copyrighting your song is a necessary step for protecting your music against plagiarism and theft.

You only have to look at some of the industry's biggest copyright dispute cases to prove the fact – George Harrison vs. the Chiffons; Robin Thicke & Pharrell Williams vs. Marvin Gaye; Vanilla Ice vs. Queen as well as more recent battles between the likes of Lana Del Rey and Coldplay.

What lesson can we learn from all of these big names? That no matter where you are in your music career - copyrighting your music gives you the exclusive rights to:

- Distribute your music in all formats, both physical and digital
- Create derivative works or samples based on your music; and
- Perform your music live [34]

If you're U.S.-based, copyrighting your music by a more official means will give you that added layer of protection if, or when, you ever find yourself in the middle of a copyright dispute. Having written what could be the next number-one song, you need to protect your song and yourself.

This involves registering your songs and music with the USCO. For U.S. artists, this has definite benefits in terms of increasing your leverage, protection, and power when it comes to making money from your music catalog.

New legislation passed in 2019 by the US Supreme Court requires all music and songs be registered with the USCO before you can file any kind of copyright dispute or infringement lawsuit.

When registering your song with the USCO, there are two forms you need to know about: Form PA & Form SR.

If you want to claim the copyright for the composition or underlying musical work, fill out Form PA (Performing Arts), available at copyright.gov/forms/formpa.pdf

---

[34] (Ditto Music, 2021)

If you want to claim the copyright for a sound recording or recorded performance; fill out Form SR (Sound Recording), available at copyright.gov/forms/formsr.pdf

NOTE: If you're the single owner of both the composition and the sound recording, you only need to fill out the SR form. You can use the authorship statement in Space 2 on the SR Form to specify that the claim covers both works.

You can print the forms out and mail them to the US Copyright Office. Or, fill out and submit an electronic application (copyright.gov/circs/circ02.pdf)

**The Costs**

There's a small filing fee for registering your songs via USCO. You can find out more information on the associated costs from the fees section of their website:

copyright.gov/about/fees.html

**Five "Easy" Steps**

1. Make a physical copy

First, write down or make a recording of your music. It sounds obvious, but the truth is, putting pen to paper or sound to recording is the first official step for claiming your music copyright – whether a song, a symphony or a jingle.

It can be as minimal as writing down your song lyrics on a piece of paper, making a note of the melody on some manuscript, or using a digital device to make a vocal or instrumental recording.

Whatever method you choose is up to you – so long as it's possible to reproduce the song that you've 'fixed' into existence through some sort of tangible format.

Why?

As soon as you've physically written it down, your song is already copyrighted. Which brings us to the second step.

2. Create timely evidence for your case

Copyright is a time-related issue. Remember the copyright dispute cases we mentioned? Whoever gets to the post office or the iCloud first is the winner.

Although you can argue that copyright exists as soon as a song or piece of music has been written down, it's better if you can prove when the tangible copy was made.

This is especially important in the case of any potential disputes about the 'originality' or 'authorship' of your work. In court, you'd be required to produce evidence that your music existed before anyone else copied it – what's known as a 'time stamped copy'.

3. File the right forms (USCO)

Now you've got a time-stamped copy of your tune, it's time to dive a bit deeper into the complex landscape of copyright.

## 4. Divide the profits

How the money is divided up between the publishing and masters is very much down to how the actual song is being used.

While you – the recording artist - will reap rewards from mechanical royalties if it's a physical sale such as a CD or vinyl, the industry standard split is 91% to the master and around 9% to the publishing.

For music sync, it's usually a 50/50 split between publishing and masters, making music sync another great avenue for new artists to explore.

NOTE: if you're a solo artist, you own all the copyright. But if you're in a band or there are multiple songwriters or co-writers, that must be included in the paperwork to make sure different portions of the copyright are fairly distributed.

## 5. Start earning money from copyright royalties

Copyright is great because it gives you full ownership rights to your music and prevents any mean people from stealing or copying your work. It also requires your permission for others to record, distribute, sample or perform your song.

Copyrighting your music opens you up to another potential revenue stream: via copyright royalty pay-outs every time someone wants to perform or use your work.

*(This might be a good time to go back and review Chapter 17 on music publishing royalties. —ed.)*

**Final copyright notes**

What's eligible for copyright

- Song lyrics
- Completed works (such as songs, jingles, incidental music, symphonic pieces)

Not eligible for copyright

- Song titles
- Chord progressions
- Incomplete or unfinished works [35]

---

[35] (Ditto Music, 2021)

## Chapter 19:

## How to Record or Demo Your Songs

Are you new to recording? If so, you may wish to start by having a very basic gear setup on a Mac laptop.

Here is a recommended home music studio setup:

1. Apple MacBook Air Laptop ($999-$1249. You can buy an older refurbished model to save some money). You can take this thin and portable laptop anywhere.

2. GarageBand. GarageBand Digital Audio Workstation (DAW) comes free with your new MacBook Air. GarageBand is excellent for beginners and provides a fully equipped music creation studio inside your Mac, complete with an extensive sound library that includes instruments, presets for guitar and voice, and an incredible selection of session drummers and percussionists.

3. PreSonus AudioBox GO audio interface ($79.99). This USB audio interface connects to your computer via a USB cable, which can also be used to connect your microphone, guitar, or music keyboard to your laptop computer.

4. A pair of PreSonus Eris E3.5-3.5" Near Field Studio Monitors ($99.99). These are great speakers for the size and price. The sound is pleasant to the ears, not too harsh, with good bass and treble response.

5. Audio-Technica AT4040 Microphone ($299.99). This is an excellent microphone, best in class, and perfect for home studios.

You may purchase a MIDI keyboard, drum machine, electric or acoustic guitar to help you create music with your music gear.

Professional songwriter Clay Mills said, "for the price of a couple demos, I had a complete recording studio with everything I needed with a simple, affordable recording set-up."

If you don't want to use a Mac laptop, there are some alternatives:

1. You can use a PC laptop with "Cakewalk by Bandlab" as a DAW (a free PC alternative to GarageBand).

2. You can use your iPad or iPhone to record and export to GarageBand on a desktop Mac.

3. You can use your Android phone or tablet with the BandLab app as a DAW (BandLab is a free Android alternative to GarageBand).

"I think it's wise and helpful to always treat your writing session like it's the recording session too," said Scott Oatley, Overall Grand Prize winner of the 2021 USA Songwriting Competition. He continued, "As an artist, that means coming in ready to throw down on the mic. Most of the time, I prefer my demo vocals to ones I record later because there is this raw energy or emotion I get in the heat of the moment that I can't recreate a week or two down the road when I finally revisit the song."

Oatley concluded, "You probably just spent hours ruminating in the depths of this song while writing it, so be smart and capture that feeling while it's still in the air."

**Picking Your Recording Method**

There are many ways to record your music these days, ranging from the extremely simple to the elaborate. What you do depends upon the time, money and recording skills you have at your disposal, but here are the main options:

1. Smart phone - either at home or in a practice studio. You can then edit the sound using an app such as GarageBand, Logic, or any other computer recording software.

2. Digital or analogue handheld recorder. These products are specifically designed to record at a high quality and are very quick and easy to use.

3. Computer software (Digital Audio Workstations) at home. You can use your computer microphone, or plug in an interface and use a higher quality microphone to record your voice and instruments. The success of this method depends a lot upon your skills. It's not difficult to record a basic demo for a soloist, but for vocals and guitar there is more you need to know. If you want to mic up a drum kit or

find a really perfect sound, you really need to be experienced to make this method work. Option 4 may be for you:

4. Hire studio space. This is a good idea if you don't feel confident recording yourself, or if you don't know anybody who can help you. It is much more expensive, but if you are well prepared, know what you want to do with your songs, and have a high budget, it's a good way to get your first recordings done.

Extra tips:

1. Decide whether to record live, or whether to use a metronome and multitrack your instruments. Some people prefer live recordings because they can capture the energy of a song more authentically, but multitracking is more accurate and allows more room for extra instrumentation.

2. Think honestly about the kind of musician you are, and try to use a method that most reflects you – if you like a grungy sound, then homemade recordings might be the best way to appeal to your fans. If you want a clean, polished sound, invest in proper equipment and engineering from the start.

# Conclusion

Start writing your song now. It doesn't have to be perfect. However, you will need to at least start writing your song.

Here's what a few award-winning songwriters have said about writing songs:

Guitarist and songwriter Christie Lenée, finalist in the 2021 Christmas Songwriting Competition, said, "The most challenging aspects of writing for me come into place with editing (re-writing). Often I have more ideas than are necessary for one song."

Lenée continued, "Likewise, I do my best to find the gems in the lyrics and melodies, find creative ways to keep those as the focus. If I notice myself using a lot of mixed metaphors or too many lyrical ideas, or if the melody is drifting too far away from the original concept, the greatest challenge is to reel it in and keep it focused. When focus remains, it seems easier for the information to be obtained later by the listener."

She added, "I am a huge fan of writing the rough draft of a song with the most basic accompaniment just to get out the ideas. Once the song starts to shape, I'll often work on the instrumental portion separately to generate the most interesting accompaniment."

"Sometimes I'll move it to another instrument (such as a 12-string guitar or piano)," she said, "or even more simply, just enhance the rhythmic patterns and chords on the guitar."

"There are times when you write a song in minutes and then there are times when it takes much longer to the point where it seems like forever," said Wilbur "B52" Levans, First Prize winner of the Hip-Hop category of the 2021 USA Songwriting Competition.

Honorable mention winner of the 2019 USA Songwriting Competition, Mary Beth Stone, said, "Once you learn the basic rules, you can experiment with breaking them. But make sure you've learned them first."

Stone added, "the quality of a song shouldn't depend on vocal harmonies and production. A really well-written song should be able to stand naked, sung with one voice and a guitar or piano. Finish the song, make it the best it can possibly be—and then dress it up with production."

The quality of a song shouldn't depend on vocal harmonies and production. A really well-written song should be able to stand naked, sung with one voice and a guitar or piano. Finish the song, make it the best it can possibly be—and then dress it up with production.

Ken Hirsch won First Prize in the Pop category of the 15th Annual USA Songwriting Competition as well as the Overall Second Prize with the song he wrote, "Is That So

Bad," co-written with Rosie Casey, Peter Roberts and Hillary Podell. Hirsch said, "It's all been said a million times but try to go with your gut and try not to compromise too much. Having said that, try to be as objective as you can. Don't fall in love with everything you write, many of the times it can be improved. Don't be reluctant to give up on an idea if it's not working."

He says he tries to separate himself from the writing, "and put myself in the place of the audience and imagine if I would enjoy listening to this song or if it moves me. And it helps to have a very thick skin, never take the rejections personally - as hard as they may be to accept, there might be a fairy tale ending just around the corner. And always keep the tape recorder running,"

Hirsch has also written numerous hit songs such as "I've Never Been to Me" by Charlene and the Top 40 hit song "Two Less Lonely People In The World" by Air Supply. His songs have been recorded by music business legends Barbara Streisand, Celine Dion and others.

Sonny King – first prize winner of the R&B category in the 2021 USA Songwriting Competition – had this to say about the recording process: "I think one final concept that has helped me throughout my career is that a song is not finished until the album or single releases to the public. I usually play all roles in the studio as writer, producer and engineer so I'm always revisiting the song in some form. I personally like to record the song and have myself and the artist live with it for a few days, maybe even a week if time permits. Let that new car smell wear off some and get past that initial feeling of 'I made a song.'"

He said, "I find that time allows me to listen to it less as "the song I made" and more like a consumer would listen. This is not a rule as sometimes a great song can come quickly. But there's nothing wrong with a few final tweaks. Just keep in mind there has to be a balance so as not to overdo it and ruin what could possibly already be good."

King continued, "You may not have the opportunity to record a song more than once in the studio but before you book that studio session, record a few rough takes on a phone or computer. Things always sound different once they are recorded. This could give you some new insight on what the song could possibly be missing."

Having read the words of people who are doing what you want to do – write music and songs – let me boil things down to four quick final pieces of advice.

## 1. Nobody is a Natural Songwriter

Songwriting is a learnable skill anyone can master given the right tools, strategies and learning. There are hit songwriters who are songwriting _teachers_ and helping budding songwriters. Seek them out.

## 2. Rewrite Your Songs

Writing songs is like creating a sculpture, a piece of art. When you return to your song an hour or a week later, you'll have forgotten some details, and that can be a very good thing.

## 3. Don't Wing It; Learn Song Structures

Learning the structures of various song styles lets you control the songwriting process so you can steer your lyrics, melody, chord progression, and rhyming structure. Do what you love, and love what you do.

## 4. Songwriting Should Come Naturally

This does _not_ contradict number 1 – "No one is a natural songwriter." If you learn the structures of songwriting—the _craft_ of being a songwriter—the momentum you build and the objections you eliminate will make your audience eager to hear your song, which always makes songwriting a more pleasant, rewarding experience.[36]

---

[36] (Brandon & Van Dyke, 5 Simple Truths I Learned About Songwriting, 2016)

*Scott Ashley*

*How To Write Better Songs*

## About the Author

Scott Ashley is a songwriter and graduate of the prestigious Berklee College of Music in Boston. He is a voting member of the Recording Academy (National Academy of Recording Arts and Sciences). He is currently working with the USA Songwriting Competition.

*Since 1995,* ***USA Songwriting Competition*** *has a long history of having winners getting recording and publishing contracts, have their songs placed on the charts as well as having their songs placed on film and television. Past winners include: David Wilcox, Priscilla Renea (Multiple Hit Songwriter for Ariana Grande, Fifth Harmony, Kelly Clarkson, etc.), American Authors (Pop/Rock Group with hits on the Billboard Charts), Alannah Myles (Grammy award winner), Ari Gold, Patrice Pike, Adrianne Gonzalez, etc. For more information on USA Songwriting Competition, visit:* [https://www.songwriting.net](https://www.songwriting.net)

*Since 2004,* ***IAMA (International Acoustic Music Awards)*** *is the preeminent awards for musicians, promotes excellence in Acoustic Music Performance and Artistry. Acoustic artists in various genres can gain exciting radio and web exposure through this competition. Win prizes in 8 different categories: Best Male Artist, Best Female Artist, Best Group/Duo, Folk, Americana/Roots/AAA, Instrumental, Open (any musical style or genre), Bluegrass/Country, etc. Past winners include: Meghan Trainor (#1 Hit on the Billboard Hot 100 Charts, 200 Album Charts and Grammy Award Best New Artist Winner), Rod*

*Scott Ashley*

*Abernethy, Ellis Paul, Jonathan Brooke, Charlie Dore (#1 on the Billboard Charts, artist from UK), The Refugees (#1 on the Billboard Charts), etc. For more information on IAMA (International Acoustic Music Awards), visit: https://www.inacoustic.com*

# Works Cited

Axel, M. (2011, August 8). *Creative Collaboration: The Power of Co-writing.* Retrieved from Songwriting Tips, News & More: https://www.songwriting.net/blog/bid/66027/Songwriting-Collaboration-The-Power-of-Co-writing

Blick, M. (2012, September 10). *Five Beatles Songwriting Tricks.* Retrieved from Songwriting Tips, News & More: https://www.songwriting.net/blog/bid/108943/5-Beatles-Secrets-about-Songwriting-I-wish-I-d-discovered-decades-sooner

Brandon, J. (2018, April 10). *7 Beatles Secrets about Songwriting I wish I'd Discovered Decades Sooner (Part 2).* Retrieved from Songwriting Tips, News & More: https://www.songwriting.net/blog/7-beatles-secrets

Brandon, J. (2018, January 7). *Top Ten tips for Entering Songwriting Competitions.* Retrieved from Songwriting Tips, News & More: https://www.songwriting.net/blog/ten-tips-entering-songwriting-competitions

Brandon, J. (2019, January 16). *How to Become a Topline Songwriter.* Retrieved from Songwriting Tips, News & More: https://www.songwriting.net/blog/how-to-become-a-topline-writer

Brandon, J. (2022, February 7). *4 Types of Royalties Involved in Music Publishing.* Retrieved from Songwriting Tips, News & More: https://www.songwriting.net/blog/4-types-of-royalties-involved-in-music-publishing

Brandon, J. (2022, January 3). *6 Tips to Help You Complete a Song.* Retrieved from Songwriting Tips, News & More: https://www.songwriting.net/blog/6-tips-to-help-you-complete-a-song

Brandon, J. (2022, March 4). *How to Write a Melody for Any Lyric.* Retrieved from Songwriting Tips, News & More: https://www.songwriting.net/blog/songwriting-tips-how-to-write-a-melody-for-any-lyric

Brandon, J. (2022, March 8). *Songwriting Secrets to Create Better Stories.* Retrieved from Songwriting Tips, News & More: https://www.songwriting.net/blog/songwriting-secrets-to-create-better-stories

Brandon, J., & Van Dyke, R. (2016, May 10). *5 Simple Truths I Learned About Songwriting.* Retrieved from Songwriting Tips, News & More: https://www.songwriting.net/blog/5truthsaboutsongwriting

Brown, R. (2022). *10 Best Music Sync Licensing Companies That Actually Deliver For Artists.* Retrieved from Omarimc.com: https://www.omarimc.com/best-music-sync-licensing-companies/

Ditto Music. (2018, May 25). *10 Songwriting Tips from the Pros.* Retrieved from dittomusic.com: https://dittomusic.com/en/blog/how-to-write-a-song-10-tips-on-how-to-boost-your-creative-side-when-writing-songs

Ditto Music. (2021, December 14). *How to Copyright a Song in 5 Simple Steps.* Retrieved from ditto.com: https://dittomusic.com/en/blog/how-to-copyright-a-song-in-5-simple-steps/

DittoMusic. (2022, May 4). *How to Write a Chord Progression Listeners Will Love.* Retrieved from dittomusic.com: https://dittomusic.com/en/blog/how-to-write-a-chord-progression-listeners-will-love

Ewer, G. (2021, March 1). *7 Ideas for Creating Chord Progressions.* Retrieved from Songwriting Tips, News & More: https://www.songwriting.net/blog/7-ideas-for-creating-chord-progressions

Indie Music Academy. (2022). *Music Royalties Explained: The Ultimate Guide for 2022.* Retrieved from Indie Music Academy:

https://www.indiemusicacademy.com/blog/music-royalties-explained

Leikin, M.-A. (2013, April 8). *The Bridge, the Whole Bridge and Nothing but the Bridge*. Retrieved from Songwriting Tips, News & More: https://www.songwriting.net/blog/bid/113522/Songwriting-Tip-Writing-The-Bridge

Murphy, R. (2017, May 18). *Focus On Your Own Strengths*. Retrieved from Songwriting Tips, News & More: https://www.songwriting.net/blog/focus-on-your-strengths

NPR. (2010, June 21). *Insider Secrets To Great Songwriting*. Retrieved from Talk of the Nation: https://www.npr.org/2010/06/21/127988439/insider-secrets-to-great-songwriting

Pollack, A. W. (2001). *Notes on "While My Guitar Gently Weeps"* . Retrieved from soundscapes.info: https://www.icce.rug.nl/~soundscapes/DATABASES/AWP/wmggw.shtml

Randle, K. (2017, February 1). *3 Uncomfortable Truths About Why Most Songwriters Never Crack Through To Success*. Retrieved from Songwriting Tips, News & More: https://www.songwriting.net/blog/3uncomfortabletruthssongwriting

Randle, K. (2020, May 11). *10 Simple Steps to Write a Song*. Retrieved June 27, 2022, from Songwriting Tips, News & More: https://www.songwriting.net/blog/10-simple-steps-to-write-a-song

Randle, K. (2020, May 1). *5 Secrets to Writing a Great Chorus*. Retrieved from Songwriting Tips, News & More: https://www.songwriting.net/blog/5-secrets-to-writing-a-great-chorus

Randle, K. (2020, April 2). *How to Write a Killer Hook*. Retrieved from Songwriting Tips, News & More: https://www.songwriting.net/blog/how-to-write-a-killer-hook

Randle, K. (2020, August 25). *Top 10 Ideas for Writing Great Melodies*. Retrieved from Songwriting Tips, News & More: https://www.songwriting.net/blog/top-10-ideas-for-writing-great-melodies

Randle, K. (2020, October 13). *Top 8 Tips To Use Rhyme To Enhance Your Lyrics*. Retrieved from Songwriting Tips, News & More: https://www.songwriting.net/blog/top-8-tips-to-use-rhyme-to-enhance-your-lyrics

Made in the USA
Coppell, TX
05 November 2024